T0329201

AFRICA:

BEYOND RECOVERY

by
THANDIKA MKANDAWIRE
London School of Economics and Political Science

The Aggrey-Fraser-Guggisberg Memorial Lectures, Series 32

UNIVERSITY OF GHANA

First published in 2015 for UNIVERSITY OF GHANA by
Sub-Saharan Publishers
P.O.Box 358
Legon-Accra
Ghana
Email: saharanp@africaonline.com.gh
Website: www.sub-saharan.com

© University of Ghana 2015
    P.O.Box LG 25
    Legon-Accra
    Ghana
    Tel: +233-302-500381
    Website:http//www.ug.edu.gh

ISBN: 978-9988-8602-0=2

Copyright Notice

AFRICA:
BEYOND RECOVERY

by
Thandika Mkandawire
London School of Economics and Political Science

The Aggrey-Fraser-Guggisberg Memorial Lectures, Series 32
Delivered on 17, 18, 19 April 2013 at the University of Ghana, Legon

THE AGGREY-FRASER-GUGGISBERG MEMORIAL LECTURES

The Aggrey-Fraser-Guggisberg Memorial Lectures were instituted in 1957 to commemorate the contribution made by the three persons memorialized to the founding of Achimota College, now Achimota School, and more generally to the advancement of education and particularly higher education in Ghana. The three persons honoured by the lectures are:

James Kwegyir Aggrey

A native of Anomabu in Ghana, Aggrey was a great African visionary and spokesman for racial harmony and equality. He was the first Vice-Principal of Achimota School. His outstanding contributions are symbolized in the shield of the school, the black and white piano keys which stand for harmony among the black and white races.

Alexander G. Fraser

The first Principal of Achimota College, Fraser was a humane, courageous and far-sighted Scottish educationist who brilliantly advocated for education in what was then the Gold Coast in the days of scepticism about the educational potential of the African.

Gordon Guggisberg

Guggisberg was perhaps the best administrator that Britain ever sent to govern a West African colony. Far in advance of the official colonial thinking of his day, he gave concrete expression to the ideals which formed the basis of Ghana's present progress. Under his vigorous sponsorship Achimota School grew to become one of the most distinguished educational institutions in Africa. Railways, major roads and a major hospital were also constructed during his tenure.

The Aggrey-Fraser-Guggisberg Lectures, given semi-annually, are a major event in the life of the University of Ghana and indeed of the country. Choice of theme and the topics to be treated are entirely up to the disgression of the lecturer, who is invariably very distinguished in his or her field of endeavour. The lectures presented here constituted the thirty-second in the series.

TABLE OF CONTENTS

LIST OF TABLES

LIST OF FIGURES

FOREWORD

The Aggrey-Fraser-Guggisberg Memorial Lectures mark the high point of the University of Ghana's calendar each year. The lecture series was established in 1957 to celebrate three men who inspired the development of higher education in Ghana. They were James Emman Kwegyir Aggrey, a Gold Coast educationist who had spent time in the United States; Alexander Gordon Fraser, the Scottish missionary; and Gordon Guggisberg, a colonial Governor of the Gold Coast, all of whom were associated with the founding of Achimota School, a symbol of public interest in high quality secondary education. The lectures in their honour have always attracted distinguished men and women as speakers. Incidentally, Arthur Lewis, the Economics Nobel Laureate, was one of the early speakers.

In 2013, the University of Ghana was fortunate to have Professor Thandika Mkandawire, the first Chair in African Development at the London School of Economics, as the distinguished Aggrey-Fraser-Guggisberg Memorial Lecturer. Professor Mkandawire spoke on the theme "Beyond Recovery" where he traced Africa's beleaguered attempts at growth and development since the independence era, the attempts at recovery and the road to sustained development.

These lectures were very well received by a very enthusiastic audience. This was largely a result of the relevance of the theme, the delivery of the lectures and the stature of the lecturer. On the relevance of the theme, it was obvious that the predicament that African countries found themselves in, as slowly developing economies with no clear indication of the best ways out of their socio-economic difficulties, made the audience anxious to know if there were new approaches to be pushed for. The basic message of the lecturer, that nations needed to look beyond recovery and think about long term structural transformation, was one to be welcomed by an audience that had become sceptical about 'fire-fighting' in the management of African economies. The delivery was very well done, and with a lot of humour.

The stature of Professor Thandika Mkandawire as a very well-known analyst of African development made the 2013 lectures very special. Professor Mkandawire has a reputation of being honest and frank in his well-researched views about Africa's political economy story. He has spent many years studying in detail the way economic decisions have been made by several countries, and has made very objective assessments of resulting policies in these economies. He has gained a great deal of respect worldwide for being forthright in debates on the political economy of African development. It was these qualities of Professor Thandika Mkandawire that prompted the University of Ghana to invite him to deliver the 2013 lectures, and the event turned out to be a great success.

This publication of the lectures delivered over three days is our way of sharing a great lecture series with the larger world that missed the opportunity to listen to them personally in 2013.

Ernest Aryeetey
Vice Chancellor, University of Ghana.

LECTURE 1

FROM RECOVERY TO DEVELOPMENT

INTRODUCTION

During the last five years or so, we have been regaled with rubrics such as "Africa Rising", "Roaring Lions", "Awakening Giant", etc. The titles of articles say it all, after years when the continent's name was associated with the most negative epithets. The doom-laden predictions are being replaced with euphoric accounts of the "lions" roaring in Africa as they chase the Asian tigers. *The Atlantic Magazine* wrote "The Next Asia is Africa: Inside The Continent's Rapid Economic Growth"; *Vogue* published a special edition on African dress, with the dapper Nigerian President as one of its models; *The Guardian* urged its readers to "Forget the Usual Tired Debates about Africa, it's Changing – For the Better"; the IPOS headlined its report at a conference in Cape Town "Africa – A Place Where You Will Make Money, Not Lose Money"; *Ventures* reported "Africa's Richest Woman Buys Portuguese Pay-Tv Company"; and a State Department press release read "Africa: Continent – The Next Frontier for Investors". Befitting the year of the Olympic Games, Paul Collier's "The Bottom Billion" (Collier, 2007) has, in other hands, morphed into the "Fastest Billion". Perhaps the most Pauline conversion has been that of *The Economist*. In May 2000, it ran a cover story: "Africa, The Hopeless Continent". In November 2011, the cover title was "Africa Rising". The magazine described the 2000 article as having "regrettably labelled Africa 'the hopeless continent' a decade ago" and claimed that "a profound change has taken hold".

I suggest that Africans should keep as far away from the "Afro-euphoria" as they did from the "Afropessimism" and assume a serene, vigilant and critical position towards events. This does seem to be happening, at least judging from the fact that Africans themselves are not out there dancing in the streets. Some have interpreted this call for caution amidst the great celebration as a new kind of Afropessimism. But it is not. It is simply a precautionary reminder that "recovery" is not the same thing as development and that we still have a long way to go.

Before we join the celebration, we need to go through a number of steps. The first of these is to understand the magnitude of the economic performance and its impact on our economies, polities and societies and its adequacy in addressing the serious problems of underdevelopment and poverty that afflict our continent. The second step is simply to understand the factors behind the recovery and the final step is to consider the sustainability of the current boom or ways of making the economic growth much higher and much more inclusive than ever.

Figure1.1: GDP per capita (Constant 2000 US$)

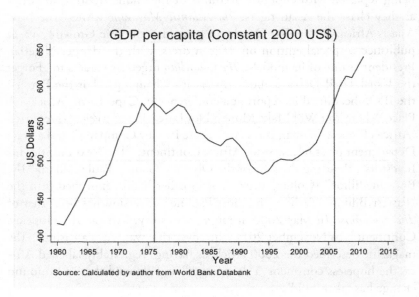

Source: Calculated by author from World Bank Databank

Table 1.1: Africa's Economic Performance, 1965–2011

Indicators	Development (1965–73)	Crisis 1974–1980	Adjustment (1981–1995	Recovery 1995-2010
1995-2010				
Re-Exports of goods and services (% of GDP)	23.3	28.4	26.3	31.3
GDP growth (annual %)	4.8	3.4	1.6	4.4
GDP per capita growth (annual %)	2.1	0.6	-1.1	1.8
Inflation, GDP deflator (annual %)	4.4	11.9	10.3	6.7
Gross capital formation (% of GDP)	22.7	25.1	19.1	18.8
Agriculture, value added (% of GDP)	20.6	19.6	18.4	16.7
Gross domestic savings (% of GDP)	21.2	23.6	17.9	15.9
Industry, value added (% of GDP)	31.0	33.8	32.5	30.1
Manufacturing, value added (% of GDP)	17.5	16.8	17.0	14.2
Trade (% of GDP)	47.9	57.7	53.6	64.2

Source: World Bank Databank.

Recovery or "Catching Up"?

Figure 1 shows Africa's growth trajectory since 1960, the modal year of "Africa's independence". We can clearly see that Africa is emerging from a deep depression (the so-called "Lost Decades") of 1980s 1990s. In its simplest formulation, the recovery refers to positive rates of economic growth during the decade and half. African economies have grown at the rate of around 5 per cent during this period, and 6 countries have been "among the top 10 fastest growing economies in the world", a recurring phrase in the euphoric account. These rates stand out in stark contrast to the poor rates of growth during the "Lost Decades" that sustained much of the Afropessimism. There may therefore be reason for celebration. However, we should recall that high growth rates are not new in Africa. Indeed, the rates of growth of the first decades in the post-colonial era compare favourably with the current ones. In 1978, not content with the growth rate of 5.7 per cent, the African Ministers of Finance requested advice from the World Bank regarding how to achieve higher rates of growth, comparable to the East Asian rate then. The World Bank's response was the famous "Berg Report" (World Bank, 1981) which outlined a dogmatic agenda that would underpin the "Lost Decades".

More significantly, we should recall that much of the growth involved recovery from the maladjustment debacle. The real challenge for Africa is not merely recovery but "accelerated development" on which the International Financial Institutions (FDIs) never delivered. In the publication that was most focussed on growth, the World Bank introduced a measure based on two criteria. The first was that the growth in the 1990s should be sufficient to indicate catching up with the USA. This suggested a growth rate of at least 1.7 per cent. In Africa, 13 countries met this criterion. The World Bank then suggested that in addition to the 1.7 per cent growth a country must have enjoyed 1 per cent growth in the 1990s. Using this criterion but considering growth between 1990 and 2011 effectively leaves 9 countries as "catch-up" cases: Equatorial Guinea, Botswana, Mauritius, Cape Verde, Burkina Faso, Lesotho, Ghana, the Seychelles and Rwanda. The other four high-growth economies were either emerging from war or beneficiaries of a resource boom. For much of Africa, the situation is one of recovery and not catch-up. The per capita income before the crisis peaked at US$577 in 1976. The peak of per capita income was only reached 30 years later in 2006 for sub-Saharan Africa as a whole. Many countries have yet to reach their individual peaks. Ghana reached its 1970 peak per capita income only in 2006.

Table1.2: Growth and "Catching Up"

	Country	Growth (1980s)	Growth (1990s)	
1	Equatorial Guinea	1.4	20.8	catching up
2	Botswana	7.9	3.9	catching up
3	Mauritius	4.9	3.8	catching up
4	Sudan	0.7	3.4	
5	Cape Verde	4.2	3.1	catching up
6	Uganda	0.5	3.1	
7	Mozambique	0.6	3.0	
8	Burkina Faso	1.4	2.5	catching up
9	Mali	1.2	2.1	
10	Lesotho	2.0	1.8	catching up
11	Ghana	1.0	1.8	catching up
12	Rwanda	1.2	1.7	catching up
13	Seychelles	2.0	1.7	catching up

Source: World Bank.

POLICY MAKERS' CLAIMS

Like for all other good things, claims to paternity were quick to arise. International financial institutions immediately argued that finally Africa was witnessing the bearing of fruit of the adjustment and stabilisation policies that were the bitter pill unavoidably imposed upon them in the 1980s. Policy makers may be so empowered by a particular idea that they will attribute to it any economic achievement. Thus, many policy makers now claim that Africa's current round of "revival" is due to "good governance", "respect for property rights", "getting prices right", etc., even when a strong case can be made that debt relief, improved terms of trade, and political stability provide a more credible explanation. After more than fifteen years of adjustment, around 1997 a number of World Bank and IMF officials staged a roadshow to proclaim that adjustment was finally working (Fischer, Hèrnandez-Catàa and Kahn, 1998; Madavo, 1997). Rejecting claims that exogenous factors may have accounted for the recovery, the IMF argued:

> The improvements in economic performance are encouraging because they cannot be explained by

exogenous developments, such as changes in the weather or favourable terms of trade. In fact the terms of trade of SSA declined at a moderate pace during 1990–94 and 1995–7. Rather the improvements resulted mainly from improved policies in a number of SSA countries." (Fischer *et al.*, 1998).

The incumbent political leaders have also claimed that it is their wisdom and astuteness that have produced the recent "miracles" that have taken place under their watch. However, most leaders would be hard pressed to point out which distinct policy or act of theirs accounts for the high growth in their respective economies.

With respect to the international institutions, the least one can say is that their claims are rather disingenuous. One can raise at least six points about their claims. As we noted above, the "Berg Report" (World Bank, 1981) promised African economies "accelerated development" if only they got their prices right. At no time had Africans been made to believe that the time lag of adjustment policies would be ten to fifteen years. The "Berg Report" was supposed to result in "accelerated growth" within a short span of time. It is clear that in earlier pronouncements, two to three years was the expected time lag. In the foreword to the World Bank's report on Africa's growth and development in the 1980s (World Bank, 1989), the World Bank's vice president for the African region bluntly stated: "Recovery has begun". The Bank's argument was that that the "positive economic trends" should be dated from 1985[1] and indeed, within a few years, the World Bank began producing league

---

1   Paul Mosley and John Weeks summarise the position of the bank thus:

(a) that economic recovery had begun and could be dated from 1985;

(b) that on balance the sub-Saharan region suffered less from external "shocks" than other regions during the 1970s and 1980s;

(c) the familiar Bank tenet that domestic policies had been and would be more important in determining performance than external factors;

(d) that structural adjustment programs, and especially those fostered by the Bank itself, had been instrumental in bringing on the putative recovery; with the corollary that countries which adopted Bank programs performed better than those which did not;

(e) that the poor gained absolutely and relatively to the rest of the population as a result of adjustment programs; and

(f) that foreign donors provided strong support for sub-Saharan countries during the 1970s and 1980s (Mosley and Weeks, 1993: 253).

tables of good and bad "performers" with respect to policy reforms. The league tables themselves were interesting for the brief duration of time in which countries featured in them before they were relegated to the group of "poor performers". Much of the "success" attributed to policy had to do with the funding that often temporarily relaxed the foreign exchange constraint and led to improved capacity utilisation. Generally, this had a one-off effect as countries fell back onto the low-growth path. Therefore, there were many "growth episodes", even during the "Lost Decades", but they were also short-lived (Hausmann, Pritchett and Rodrik, 2005). However, since there were no definite indicators of the time lag between policy and recovery, it could always be argued that the "Lost Decades" were indeed the true time lag for the impact of policy reforms.

The second point was that there was considerable academic literature suggesting that IMF policies lead to poor growth rate (Bird and Row-lands, 1997, Przeworski and Vreeland, 2000, Sender, 1999, Stein, 2004, Weisbrot, Naiman and Kim, 2000).

The third point is that by the mid-1980s the IFIs and economists associated with them began to suggest a range of explanations that weak-ened the policy arguments of central structural adjustments and their conditionalities. By 1989, the failure to "get prices right" and the mac-roeconomic model underpinning it had already led to a new search for the determinants of Africa's poor performance. In 1989, the World Bank identified "governance" as the problem (World Bank, 1989). The Webe-rian language of the report did not fit well with the dominant neoclassical paradigm and the focus on "governance" was seen as a distraction from the more serious task of getting prices right and reducing the role of the state in the economy. It was only with the emergence of new institution-alism, especially through the seminal work of Douglas North, that "get-ting institutions right" was given a rational choice framework compatible with the epistemological framework of the Washington Consensus. In addition, as both market and institution reforms did not seem to yield the expected result, new studies emerged suggesting that exogenous factors rather than policy accounted for Africa's poor performance. Now, blame was placed on Africa's colonial historical legacy (Acemoglu, Johnson and Robinson, 2001, Bolt and Bezemer, 2008, Price, 2003), on its ethnic di-versity (Easterly and Levine, 1995), on its unfavourable geography (poor soils, tropical bugs) (Collier and Gunning, 1999), on mistimed "demo-graphic transition", on African culture and the "neopatrimonialism" it spawned (Bach, 2011, Van de Walle, 2001), on its boundaries, which rendered many counties landlocked or conflict-prone (Collier and Gunning, 1999) , on its natural resources (the resource curse), etc. (Sachs and Andrew, 1997). And to top it off, the World Bank, the driver of much of the reform agenda in Africa, began to attribute the negative effects of its policies or the failure of its policies to external factors:

> There is little doubt that the 1980s—the "lost" decade— had its share of negative shocks, including declines in primary commodity prices, a collapse in oil prices, a sharp hike in U.S. interest rates, debt crises, a sudden stop in capital flows to developing countries, and a collapse in import demand from developing countries. (World Bank, 2004: 63).

For an institution that had, for much of the 1980s and 1990s, insisted on internal factors as the cause of the "Lost Decade", this was quite a climb-down. One would expect that in light of this the dramatic improvements in the external environment would loom large in explanations for the recovery.

This recourse to all these exogenous factors, such as geography, culture, and history, of course, produced a dilemma for the policy peddlers. Obviously, the more is attributed to these factors, the less agency plays an important role in development. These historical and exogenous factors left little room for policy explanations. Nevertheless, in their more political pronouncements, World Bank officials still insisted that "improved macroeconomic policies" produced the recovery.

The fourth point to note is that advocates of the Washington Consensus argued that the failure of their policies was due to recidivism and non-compliance with the prescribed policies. Two reasons were suggested for this non-compliance – one was internal and another external, both involving clientelism. One was self-interest, which blocked the reforms that would undermine rent-seeking activities and the clientelism associated with. The external reason was that the political conditionalities of the donors trumped the economic conditionalities. Political clients or allies were often treated more leniently at the behest of the "principals" of the IMF, thus undermining the IMF's capacity to enforce its conditionalities (Stone, 2004). Thus, apparently, the failure of structural adjustment programmes was due to non-implementation of advice from the IFI. It would therefore be odd to attribute the recovery to unimplemented policies, but even if one wanted to push the point about recidivism by arguing that it did not apply to all, one would have to establish the difference in performance between the "strong adjusters" and the "weak adjusters" of the 1990s. In 1994, the World Bank published a classification of African countries that distinguished strong adjusters from non-adjusters. One expectation then would be that the former would outperform the non-adjusters in the subsequent years. There is no evidence of such better performance. It could, of course, be that during the last fifteen years all African countries improved their policy indicators or that there had been high levels of recidivism on the part of strong adjusters. This, however, can be interpreted as evidence of the endogeneity of the policy measures themselves. With economic recovery, many indicators, such as the fiscal position of the government and the balance of payments, have improved. In light of all this, it is difficult to see the link between orthodox policies and economic performance.

The fifth point is the expressions of doubts about the efficacy of the model by the Washington institutions themselves. In the case of Africa, the World Bank was constrained to state:

> The failure of growth in Africa—either of powerful and rapid growth in a single large country or in a substantial number of smaller ones—was a surprise. Despite good policy reforms, debt relief, continued high levels of official assistance, promising developments in governance, and a relatively supportive external climate, no take-off has ensued.
>
> If, as suggested by the growth regressions, policies matter for growth, policy improvements should lead to higher growth. Both in the 1980s and 1990s, policies improved relative to other decades, but growth performance remained well below that of the 1960s and 1970s ... More recently, empirical research has argued that when a measure of "institutional quality" is included in cross-country regressions, the explanatory power of other variables, including all measures of "policies," becomes negligible ... This suggests that "good" institutions matter more for growth than "good" policies—that "institutions rule". (World Bank, 2005: 3).

In 2008, the World Bank declared that "nobody really believes in the Washington Consensus anymore" (cited in Caldentey, 2008).

Finally, there were admissions by the IFIs themselves that, by errors of omission or commission, their policies had harmed African economies. The early 1990s produced an onslaught of studies indicating what had gone wrong during the adjustment. Let me discuss just a few here. It was in the midst of dissecting this "African tragedy", utterances of *mea culpa* and disarray that the recovery began. It would require huge amounts of institutional amnesia then to argue the result of the reforms. With the dramatic recovery of African economies, these "*mea culpas*" have been forgotten. It is, however, my contention that the aggregate impact of these errors is still present in many ways. I believe that we have to take these *mea culpa* seriously because in many ways they shaped the African economies that emerged after 15 years of failed policies. Collectively, they produced economies with peculiar and troublesome features that are affecting the capacities of the African countries to exploit the favourable conditions that have emerged. I will return to this issue later.

FACTORS BEHIND THE RECOVERY

The arguments raised above beg for an explanation of the factors behind the recovery. Here we will only highlight some of the factors, which have played out differently in different countries.

Political changes

A case can be made that political changes have impacted positively on African economies. The end of military rule in general and the resurgence of movements for democracy have placed the question of development high on the policy agenda and have made economic performance a source of legitimacy for African states. African leaders tout their economies' growth rates as a measure of their leadership. The success of leaders, even in the remaining authoritarian cases, is no longer measured by the longevity of their reign and even less so the number of medals on their chests but by the economic performance of their respective countries and the stability of their political order. This may be the single most potentially resilient change of circumstances behind the turnaround. There is today positive rivalry among African states around economic issues and an expectation by a better-informed middle class of seeing their country perform as well as its neighbours, if not better. This changed mind-set is an important prerequisite for thinking about developmental states. One effect of democratisation and greater accountability to local constituencies is that the external actors have lost traction. These political changes are no small matter, given the fact that we had leaders whose political aspirations never rose beyond the satisfaction of a few local clients and external masters who underwrote their reign.

Terms of trade

For all the talk about "opening up", African economies rely heavily on trade for their economic performance. Generally, African countries grow rapidly during periods of improved terms of trade. They did so in the booms towards the end of colonial rule (the Korean War boom) and in the booms during the interventionist era. This relationship is captured graphically in Figure 1.2. Not surprisingly, the changes in the terms of trade have played an important role in the current recovery. Over the period 1995–2006, the export values in Africa increased considerably, by 12 per cent per annum, a rate of growth that was higher than either the world or the developing-country average (Table 1.2).

There are some features of the current favourable terms of trade that must be borne in mind. First, the size of the price increases is unprecedented and unlikely to last; second, the boom covers a wide range of commodities; and, third, the boom has lasted much longer than previous ones. Furthermore, and more disturbingly, the expansion in export earnings has been based on increased prices rather than increased volumes. In other words, the growth in export values was due to rising prices rather than to increased export volumes. The price of a unit of exports increased by a yearly average of 6 per cent in Africa over the period 1995–2006 – four times higher than the world average and nearly three times higher than the developing-country average. UNCTAD had this to say:

> In summary, it appears that the notable increase in export values over the period 1995–2006 was driven largely by recent price increases rather than volume increases. The low volume effect indicates weak export response following trade liberalization. Instead, it is only the rise in world export prices, over which African countries have little control, which has allowed African exports to perform better than those of the rest of the world in value terms (UNCTAD, 2008).

Figure1.2 Terms of Trade and Growth in Sub-Saharan Africa

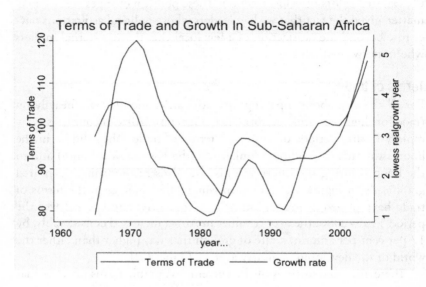

Table1.3 :Average yearly increases in merchandise export values, volumes, and prices, 1995–2006 (percentages)

	Total export value	Total export volume	Export price	unit
World	8.15	6.50	1.48	
Developing countries	11.53	9.03	2.13	
Africa	12.44	5.82	6.14	
Developing Asia	11.64	9.91	1.39	
Latin America	10.89	7.46	3.20	

Source: (2008).

There is persuasive literature restating the classical observation from economists such as Prebisch that sustained economic growth requires diversified exports. Trade liberalisation has failed to induce export diversification and has, instead, led to higher levels of export concentration in a number of countries *(see* Table 1.4).

Table1.4: Comparative export concentration indices by region, 1995 and 2011

	1995	2011
Africa	0.24	0.43
Africa excluding South Africa	0.34	0.51
Latin America	0.09	0.13
Asia	0.09	0.12
Low-income developing economies	0.14	0.25

Source: (UNECA, 2012).

Neighbourhood effect

Not all African countries may have benefitted from improved terms of trade, but it is clear that the "contagion effect" has spread some of the benefits to their neighbours. For one, the herd instincts of capitalists may have interpreted well-being in a number of key countries as indicative of the entire continent's well-being. The "Africa rising" narrative is evidence of this generalisation.

Linking up to dynamic economies

The colonial heritage of most African economies was that they were tethered to slow-growing economies. To make things worse, most of the special arrangements that Africans made with their erstwhile colonial masters, such as the Lome Convention, simply reinforced the low-growth export model. During the last decade, the share of African exports to Asia has more than doubled to 27 per cent. There is definitely evidence that economic growth in a number of countries can be attributed to Asia's demand for natural resources (Breisinger and Thurlow, 2008, Carmody, 2009).

Natural resource-driven investments

The primary sector remains the most important destination for Foreign Direct Investment (FDI) flows into the region. One driving factor has been investment in infrastructure linked to mining during the adjustments, which produced two FDI spurts. The first, which may be related to policy, was associated with market liberalisation and privatisation. Within the continent, the distribution of FDI flows is uneven, with Morocco, Angola, Equatorial Guinea, Nigeria, and Sudan accounting for more than 50 per cent of the inflows from major investors to Africa over the period 1996-2000. Within the primary sector, oil and gas are the most important.

Special drivers of FDI

The FDI that can be directly associated with policy was that attracted by the privatisation programmes of the 1990s, which naturally tapered off. Technological change has played an important role in stimulating investment. Many of the new investments are driven by the factors that account for the growth, as indicated above. Two particular factors are worth mentioning. The first of these is the investment directed towards mining. The second one is technology – driven by information and communications technology. More than 50 per cent of FDI investment in Africa over the decade 1996-2006 was in telecoms *(see* Table 1.5), showing the importance of mobile telephony in developing countries (UNCTAD, 2008b).

One must also consider here investment in the financial sector, a reflection of the excessive financialisation of African economies, and retail, as symbolised by the shopping malls that have mushroomed all over Africa.

Debt relief – the end of the debt overhang

Many studies on African growth had for years suggested that the "debt overhang" was negatively affecting investment and growth. Not surprisingly, one of the most important exogenous shocks was debt relief. The Highly-Indebted-Poor-Country (HIPC) Initiative and the Multilateral Debt Relief Initiative (MDRI) reduced the debt in 33 countries by US$43 billion. It may be that to escape from debt countries had to adopt SAP, but that does not mean it was a necessary condition for the translation of that debt relief into growth. Indeed it can be argued that the policies accompanying the debt relief have attenuated the full benefits of such relief by their deflationary bias, by limiting the capacity of the state and by inducing increased consumption in the absence of any prioritisation in the use of the released funds.

Demise of the Washington Consensus and more policy space

Finally, one should consider the reduced traction of the "Washington Consensus" and its deflationary stance. Not only has the "consensus" lost its intellectual bearing following the crisis of neoliberalism in the metropolitan countries, but the improved foreign exchange reserves of many countries has tended to undermine the conditionality-enforced policy regime. Here one should add the "China factor". The entrance of new aid donors, such as China and India, which have no particular commitment to the "consensus" that the main donors have wielded over the years, has reduced the demand for aid from the IFIs and undercut their leverage. More significantly, it has allowed governments to move away from the grip of deflationary policies and to begin to think about "growth and development" as the central preoccupations of policies in poor countries.

MEA CULPA AND THE CONSEQUENCES

We noted above that policy errors have been admitted, albeit in a backhanded way and without spelling out the full implications of the errors. What has generally been sidestepped or swept under the carpet are the "hysteresis" effects of such policies. This refers to a phenomenon observed in some physical systems, by which changes in a property lag behind changes in an agent on which they depend, so that the value of the former at any moment depends on the manner of the previous variation of the latter. In a similar way, there is "path dependence" of the state of economic variables on the past history of the economic system or policies so that policy failures in the recent past can continue to have an effect on the performance of the economy long after the policy failures have been corrected. In the current euphoric stance, the tendency has been to let bygones be bygones: not to dwell too much on the past and instead focus on the future. There is no recognition by the IFIs that their own self-confessed mistakes and failures may have far-reaching implications and that their short-term policies may have many unintended, albeit far from unpredictable, consequences for the future performance of African economies. The usual procedure has been to admit the errors and then to argue that Africans must look ahead without addressing some of the consequences of maladjustment. This is easily said, especially when one does not have to pay for the consequences. The "recovery" has allowed the IFIs to sweep these *mea culpa* under the proverbial carpet and even to claim that their policies were finally working, with a time lag of two decades!

Weakening the state

One of the most obvious errors was the devastating erosion of state capacity produced by reckless downsizing of the state through formulaic retrenchment, demoralising the civil service, and massive interference by poorly coordinated donors and, in the process, undermining the legitimacy of local political and bureaucratic actors by assuming "ownership". The view of the IFI was that African countries had bloated civil services. As it turned out, Africa has the lowest number of civil servants per 100 citizens – around 1 or fewer as compared with around 5 in other developing countries. Interestingly, it was Mauritius and Botswana that attained those figures. All in all, Africa is the least-governed place on earth.

An Independence Evaluation Group (IEG) summary of capacity building in the agriculture sector in Africa stated that:

> although some success has been achieved in implementing structural adjustment programs with a consequent reduction in government activities to a more manageable size and liberalization of economic policies that improved resource allocation and producer incentives, there has been less success in reviving the capacity of public institutions. (IEG, 1999: 2).

The bank itself blamed African countries for being "overzealous" in the reduction of the civil service.

Besides the downsizing of state institutions there were also major reforms in the administrative apparatus of the state, often along the New Management lines. Much of the institutional reform involved enhancing the power of institutions designed to limit the discretionary power of the state (independent central banks, courts, police, accounting tribunals) as opposed to the denigrated "spending ministries" This often led to the one-size-fits-all approach that drastically reduced the remit of institutions in the development (Mkandawire, 2009).

Similarly, the wrong sequencing of privatisation before there was proper regulatory capacity led to cannibalisation of the state and national patrimony and the creation of new monopolies. In addition, it contributed to the lowering of the extractive capacity of the state. One of the most disturbing outcomes of that turn of events has been the failure to capture the mineral rents during the current boom In many cases, such as Zambia, the privatisation led to enormous loss to the country as a whole as it was coerced to accept terms on taxation and revenue sharing that left virtually nothing to Zambia. The case of Zambia was so extreme that even the IMF called for an upward revision of the royalties.

Given its focus on retrenchments and assignment to the state of only a regulatory role, adjustment policies discouraged public investment on a number of grounds. First was the ideological aversion to state intervention in general. The argument against public investment was on grounds that (a) better utilisation of the existing infrastructure would be enough and that the private sector was better able to achieve this, hence the need for privatisation of public utilities; (b) public investment "crowded out" the private sector; and (c) with appropriate market signals, investment by the private sector would replace the state as an investor.

Over and above all this has been the loss of sovereignty. The grip that international organisations have had on Africa was unprecedented. Indeed, the extent to which donors controlled African economies became an embarrassment to them and they began fretting about "ownership" and "partnership".

From development to stabilisation

Even more significantly, the state was effectively removed from the development policy arena. Not only could it not pursue national development policies in any planned way, but it was removed even from the pursuit of sectoral policy.. The constraints on sectorial policy were confined not only to industry but also to agriculture, in which the only policy was "getting prices right". The conclusion of the IEG was unequivocal on this point: "the Bank has had limited success in contributing to the development of African agriculture. The neglect of infrastructure reduced economic responsiveness" (Independent Evaluation Group (IEG), 2007: xxiii).

Human capital

The low investment was not only in physical infrastructure but in human capital as well, which is impacting on Africa's capacity to exploit the current opportunities, including the "demographic dividend". Related to the non-developmental agenda were the negative view about tertiary education and the dubious argument regarding the rates of return for primary education being higher than for university education, which led to dramatic shifts of resources away from tertiary education. Years later came the *mea culpa*, albeit in a backhanded way as the World Bank switched positions, arguing now that "neglecting tertiary education could seriously jeopardize longer-term growth prospects of SSA countries" (World Bank, 2009). I will discuss this in the third lecture.

Poor infrastructure

We noted above that the state was restrained from investment in basic "public goods" on grounds that the reduction of public investment would "crowd in" private investment. As a consequence during the period of structural adjustment, there was little public investment in infrastructure. The "crowding in" "crowding out" argument notwithstanding, many of the cuts in public investment were undertaken as part of fiscal adjustment and in line with the ideologically driven reducing the role of the state in the economy. In the event, investment from the private sector was not forthcoming in the sector with the exception of the technology-driven investment in the telecommunications or mining-related infrastructure. As one IMF document observed:

> Since the private sector has not increased infrastructure investment as hoped for, significant infrastructure gaps have emerged in several countries. These gaps may adversely affect the growth potential of the affected countries and limit targeted improvements in social indicators. Not only are the governments of these countries now seeking to reverse the declining trend of public investment, partly through increased resort to private-public partnerships (PPPs), but also multilateral development banks (MDBs) have signalled that they are prepared to redirect some of their lending to infrastructure projects, to help to close infrastructure gaps." (IMF, 2004: 5).

The multilateral development banks now began to look favourably at public investment. Even the IMF began to acknowledge that the "possibility that a declining share of public investment in GDP could have adverse consequences for economic growth over the longer term is a legitimate concern, although the empirical evidence in this area is inconclusive" (IMF cited in Akyüz, 2006). It now argued that "while maintaining a focus on the overall balance and public debt as a basis for fiscal analysis and policy and fiscal conditionality in Fund-supported programs, steps are taken to promote productive public investment" (IMF, 2004).

A major cause of the poor response of African economies to opportunities has been the neglect of infrastructure, a point highlighted by African governments from the early years of adjustment, emphasised greatly by much African research and highlighted by the Commission for Africa report (Commission for Africa, 2005: 225-6). Eventually, the World Bank discovered that its dogmatic faith in the private sector would not work as throughout the developing world the private sector was unlikely to finance more than a quarter of the major infrastructure investment needs (Estache, 2005: 21). Foreign direct investment in infrastructure has been largely confined to telecoms or mining-related infrastructure (*see* Table 1.5). We should bear in mind that a considerable amount of investment was made for acquisition rather than addition of new capacity.

Table 1.5: Foreign investment commitments in the infrastructure industries in Africa, in US dollars

Sub-sector	1996–2000	2001–2006
Energy	6,837	5,724
Telecoms	11,502	13,966
Transport	1,264	5,544
Water	88	239
	19,691	25,473

UNCTAD

The low levels of investment are already proving a major bottleneck to further investment in other sectors. African countries face serious power shortages. The consequences of the neglect of infrastructure is summarised by UNCTAD and UNIDO thus:

The inadequate and poor quality of infrastructure in Africa is a major obstacle to the development of competitive industries in the region. It is estimated that Africa loses 1 percentage point per year in per capita economic growth as a result of its infrastructure deficit. The infrastructure problem is evident in areas such as power, water supply, transport and communications, which are critical to the successful development of manufacturing enterprises. Furthermore, the problem is not limited to poor network coverage but also manifested in the exceptionally high price of infrastructure services in Africa relative to global standards (Table 1.6). The high cost of infrastructure in Africa increases trade costs and reduces productivity of African firms by about 40 per cent. (UNCTAD/UNIDO, 2011).

Non-developmental financial sector

Other errors were in financial reforms, which have been misinterpreted as simply a question of wrong sequencing, taking place before fiscal consolidation; in the same vein, it has been admitted that financial liberalisation before proper regulatory institutions led to fragmentation, financial chaos including the collapse of a number of banks and high levels of non-competitive behaviour accounting for the wide gaps between interest received for savings and that for borrowing. The reformed financial sector does not mobilise savings and does not allocate savings productively. The privatised financial sector was also seen not to allocate funds productively. Much of the credit was directed towards speculative investments in real estate and consumption.

The premature opening of capital accounts

One of the demands placed on African countries was that they had to liberalise their capital accounts. One immediate effect was to increase drastically the volatility of these economies. There have been quite a number of consequences of this approach. One is high interest rates to avoid capital flight and related to that is an obsessive focus on foreign exchange reserves that is leading in many countries to an excessive accumulation of foreign reserves justified in precautionary terms to deal with some of the consequences of the policies.

Simultaneously decontrolling two inherently volatile market systems – for external capital movements and internal financial instruments – is an explosive policy mix.

Financial instability was often centred on stock markets which have been created to accompany public enterprise privatization. This fragility is exacerbated by violent movements of capital in and out of the local economy via a liberalized external capital account. (Taylor, 1997).

The holding of such excess reserves is costly on poor countries inducing them to be capital exporters.[2] The outcome is captured by UNCTAD thus:

> Between 1995 and 1998, while total SSA imports rose by some 8 per cent, reserves grew by some 50 per cent. The shift appears to be related to the liberalization of the capital account and to external financial vulnerability; five countries with the highest rates of reserve accumulation in the 1990s (Egypt, Kenya, Mauritius, Morocco and Uganda) are also the countries with more liberal capital account regimes. Given that growth in most countries in the region is constrained by the balance of payments, tying up international purchasing power through reserve accumulation entails considerable opportunity costs in terms of imports, investment and growth forgone. (UNCTAD, 2000).

Low levels of investment

The effect of wrong financial reforms, the opening of capital accounts and lowered extractive capacity of the state has been low levels of investment, despite some recovery. Considering the importance of mining and technology in telecoms in the revival of foreign direct investment, the implication is that investment in other sectors, such as agriculture and manufacturing, was too low to sustain the structural transformation of Africa's economies and exports. The investment and domestic savings rates are an additional source of weakness. The investment rates in the early 1960s averaged between 7 per cent and 8 per cent of the GDP, rising to a high point of about 13 per cent during 1975–80 before falling back to about 7.5 per cent during 1990–95. Starting in the second half of the 1990s, they have risen slowly and are currently still far below the peak of the 1970s (*see* Figure 1.3).

---

2. On the costs of excess reserves see (Cruz and Walters, 2008, Mezui and Duru, 2013, Ramachandran, 2006, Rodrik, 2006).

Figure 1.3: Investment as Share of GDP

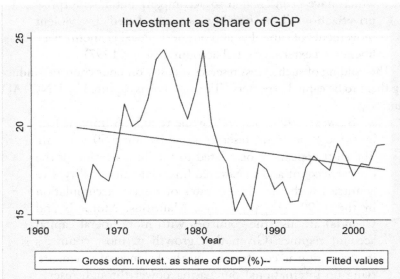

Investment as Share of GDP

Deindustrialization and the failure of diversification

One widespread consequence of the failed policies was the deindustriali-sation of the continent. Policies about "infant industries" that had stayed as infants were drawn from the Indian and Latin American experiences and applied to Africa, which had been industrialised for less than a de-cade when the crisis struck. Quite remarkably, this current commodity boom has not been accompanied by any attempts to industrialise or re-suscitate industries that had been hit by the wave of deindustrialisation. As UNIDO observed, the 1990s was marked by a shift of manufacturing out of Africa, with the notable exception of gains in South Africa as the consequence of the industrial recovery mainly in South Africa (UNIDO, 2009: 42).

One interesting difference between the two booms is that the cur-rent boom has a low income elasticity of manufacturing. In the current recovery, 1 per cent growth in GDXP leads to 1 per cent growth in man-ufacturing, compared with 1.3 per cent during the 1960–80 period (see Table 6).

Table 1.6: Income elasticity of the manufacturing industry

Variables	1960–80	1995–2010
Loggdp	1.271***	1.015***
	(-0.0318)	(-0.02520
Constant	-8.270***	-2.825***
	(-0.704)	(-0.577)
Observations	232	572
Number of countries	21	42

Notes: Calculated by the author from the World Bank Data Catalog.

The lack of structural transformation shows up in many ways. The first of these is the failure of diversification and volatility of African exports. Over the ten-year period of the recovery, the African export structure has undergone little change. The improved terms of trade have stimulated investment in mining and further deepened the mono-cultural characteristic of African economies. UNCTAD reports:

> In the period following trade liberalization, the export concentration index for Africa increased by 80 per cent, from a value of 0.21 in 1995 to 0.38 in 2006. This implies that African countries have become increasingly dependent on a limited number of commodities, in comparison with other developing regions (UNCTAD, 2008a)

Thus, Zambia has seen its copper mining rise as a share of total exports, and Ghana has once again taken on the mantle of "Gold Coast" as gold accounts for a large share of its exports.

Unresolved agrarian crisis

A major promise of adjustment was that it would reverse Africa's agriculture production and, even more significantly, bring about a reversal in food availability *(see* Figure 1.4). However, the per capita food availability remains way below the average levels of the pre-crisis years. The poor response of farmers to price incentive in the context of severe structural constraints was a major concern of development economics which was was immediately side-lined by the "Get Prices Right" dogma of the "Berg Report". However the poor response even in the face of escalating food prices has pointed to the fact that this was the consequence of a number of issues: the first of these was the collapse of the rural infrastructure. The second was the collapse of marketing boards, which have not been adequately replaced by the private sector. The third was the low levels of research and extension services.

Figure 1.4: Food Production Per Capita

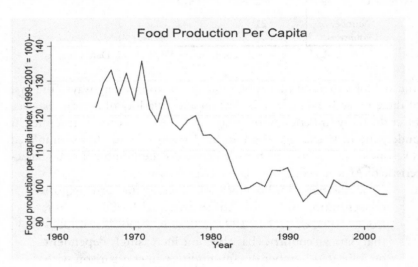

NEW CHALLENGES AND OPPORTUNITIES

Ideational shifts

A major driver of development is ideational. This involves the vision that key actors in society hold about their country's economy and the future to which they aspire. It is also ideas and ideology that sanction the instruments that can be deployed in a particular country. Developmental states have generally been driven by an idea of "catching up". The understanding of how markets work and societies are constituted and ideological predilections have determined the role that is assigned to the state, society, and markets.

Greater awareness in Africa of lagging behind

Perhaps the most negative aspects of the era of adjustment were the lowering of our vision. The short-termism that the macroeconomic policies lent to policy making still blurs the visions of African states. The hold that the finance ministry has on poverty and the weakness of planning institutions and the so-called "spending ministries" have not been relaxed by the greater access to resources.

The first is Africans' greater awareness of how much they lag behind in terms of economic performance and compelling evidence of the effectiveness of deliberate attempts to "catch up" as demonstrated by East Asian economies. Despite many attempts to present the East Asian experience as evidence of the advantages of "market friendliness", East Asia has been quintessentially interventionist. Its stellar performance has rightly been attributed to "developmental states" (Amsden, 1985, Evans, 1995, Wade, 1991, Woo-Cumings, 1999). Not surprisingly, there is great interest in "learning from the East".[3] For much of the 1960s and early 1970s, many African economies were performing as well as, if not better than, the East Asian economies in terms of economic growth and there appeared then to be little need to look to the East. It was only towards the end of the 1970s when East Asian economies ramped up their growth rates that African countries began to be interested in the East Asian experience. Indeed, it was interest in this performance that led African directors at the World Bank to seek ways to raise their growth rates (above 5 per cent during the previous decade) to the new East Asian level. The response of the World Bank was the "Berg Report", which completely contradicted the East Asian model with its anti-statism and its fetishisation of the market.

Vast amounts of research and Africa's direct interaction with the "East" have changed thinking about the Asian experience and the role of the state, with a number of leaders openly aspiring to transform their anaemic states into developmental states. Indeed, we now have a number

---

3. Unfortunately much of the "learning" is being done on behalf of Africans and filtered through paradigmatic frameworks that obscure much that is useful from that experience.

of African states with policy regimes that draw greatly on the literature and practices of developmental states.

One of the most important lessons learned from the "Lost Decades" was the importance of markets as institutions of exchange and the allocation of resources in "mixed economies" and the importance of macroeconomic issues other than growth. Earlier development economics paid little attention to macroeconomic instability except as an outcome of trade cycles. Development economics focussed on the long run and the Keynesian problematic of demand management was seen as a concern for advanced countries. We have learned that booms and busts and normal aspects of capitalist economics have to be carefully managed even in developing countries focussed on long-term growth.

In our discovery of the market, however, the conflation of being "pro-market" with "pro-business" has arisen. These are not the same developmental states that have had a pro-active relationship with business with carrots and sticks. The Washington Consensus tended to see such intervention in the language of rent-seeking and "market distortions" and therefore could not accommodate "pro-business" policies. This was capitalism of free markets without the state or capitalists.

The collapse of the Washington Consensus

Countries need policy space not only to craft policies that are appropriate to their circumstances, whether these are the constellation of political forces or resource endowments, but also to give meaning to "democratic choice" and to allow room for "learning and doing". "Catching up", by definition, means "leapfrogging", so many entirely new and unprecedented "jumps" will be required. Such a process is inherently characterised by "trial and error" and therefore requires space for experimentation. The recognition of such "trial and error" is now widespread in the literature of institutions when it looks beyond the "one-size-fits-all" view of institutions and recognises the implications of path dependence, context specificity and the political economy of change (Chang and Evans, 2000, Evans 2004). For more than a decade, African policy making was limited to a narrow space prescribed by the "Washington Consensus". Things are changing now, facilitated by the collapse of the "Washington Consensus" and its utter failure to lead to the "accelerated development" promised by the Berg Report. The IFIs, with their "damaged brand", have made some significant retreats from certain dogmatic positions about the role of the state in development and the nature of market failure in developing countries.[4] One should add here the "China factor", which, in the case of Africa, has brought in new actors who accept more state interventionist policies, or at least do not contest them. However one should not underestimate the residues of the paradigm in African policy-making circles. It is in the nature of periphery societies that old ideas from the centre may persist simply through inertia, "institutional hysteresis", the zealotry of new converts and rootedness and institutionalisation over time.

In addition, the more favourable foreign exchange positions of African governments have reduced the effectiveness of conditionalities. Historically, African states have tended to adopt expansive and at times developmental initiatives when the hold of the donors on their economies has been weakened by favourable terms of trade. The significant improvement in terms of trade has dramatically increased the policy space of many African countries although some have yet to learn how to exploit this space.

The quest for developmental institutions

As we noted above, the past agenda on institutional reform was aimed at creating a "watchman state", the function of which was merely regulatory and which was denied any entrepreneurial or transformative role. Whatever is the nature of past commitments to development, one can safely say that today there are many factors that favour a more developmentalist role for the state. For one there lively debates within Africa about developmental states.. These debates are taking place during a phase of a boom and relative peace on the continent. What matters about development is the intentionality and deliberateness of the modern development process. Some with a bellicist turn of mind have interpreted the threat of war as the driver of western industrialisation. There are no wars compelling states to mobilise resources and no dangers of fragmentation either due to conquest or due to secessionism. From this, others have suggested that African states do not face the kind of pressures that were behind

---

4 By 1997 the World Bank was compelled to concede "that development requires an effective state, one that plays a catalytic, facilitating role, encouraging and complementing the activities of private businesses and individuals". The bank concludes that "state-dominated development has failed. But so has stateless development (...). History has repeatedly shown that good government is not a luxury but a vital necessity" (World Bank, 1997b).

the strengthening of states elsewhere (Herbst, 2004; Herbst, 1990). The history of many developmental states is that they emerged to address the dire situation in which they found themselves. South Korea was a ravaged economy that had to develop rapidly and equitably if only to address the threat from the North; Mauritius was an island faced with the Malthusian threat of overpopulation and social tension in the absence of new employment opportunities; Botswana was a drought-stricken "protectorate" that was so poor that its capital (Francistown) was actually in another country. Other drivers of developmental states have been the nationalist resentment of "backwardness", non-military rivalry with neighbours, emulation and the need for industrialisation.

The literature on developmental states has identified three key features of such states: the adhesion to a "developmentalist ideology" and notions or aspirations of "catching up"; the political ability to make their ideology and developmentalist project hegemonic or, at least, embedded in society at large; and a capacity to mobilise and allocate national resources unencumbered by particularistic and short-term preoccupations. Neopatrimonialism, which is said to be pervasive in Africa, undermines all three of these elements. I have challenged these views in a number of papers.

The developmental state has generally been identified *ex post*. Developed states are not fully formed as such. They are built over many years by trial and error, intelligent emulation and borrowing, new country-specific innovations, etc., often producing a rather tautological developmental state than one that produces development.

For latecomers, the "developmental role" of institutions is central. After years of touting the Asian economies as evidence of the effectiveness of policies advocated by the Bretton Woods Institutions (BWIs), in 1993, the World Bank finally accepted the overwhelming evidence that the state had played a central role in the developmental experiences of these countries and that credit rationing and the allocation of rents had been central to the search for instruments (World Bank, 1993). However, this concession to the Asian experience was immediately set aside, at least as far as Africa was concerned. First, it was argued that "the fact that interventions were an element of some Asian economies' success does not mean that they should be attempted everywhere, nor should they be used as an excuse to resist needed market-reform" (World Bank, 1993: 23). This view was buttressed by a number of academic publications that suggested the impossibility of a developmental state in Africa (Mkandawire, 2001).

Democratisation and the demands of the middle classes

One of the drivers of better economic performance has been the middle classes, who seek better education for their children, better health facilities, and a more reliable infrastructure, and the newly empowered voters who demand accountability from the state. The relationship between the positions of the middle class and development is contradictory, swinging between aversion to state intervention and its redistributive policies and calls for a strong state, if only to provide social infrastructure and maintain "law and order". In addition, even the popular classes may share the anti-statism of "neoliberal neopopulism" (Weyland, 2004) with its incessant harping about corruption, clientelism, or inefficiency.

The stereotypical developmental state has been "bureaucratic authoritarian". From this feature of countries such as South Korea, Taiwan, and, earlier, Brazil and the poor performance of the "world's largest democracy" (India) with its miserly "Hindu rate of growth", an inference was drawn that this was a necessary feature of a developmental state. The path taken by Taiwan and Korea – first development and then democracy – supports earlier political assertions about the social and economic prerequisites of democracy as adumbrated seminally by Seymour Lipset (1959) and, until late in the 1980s, backed by many econometric studies. The paucity of "democratic developmental states" has been a striking feature of the literature on developmental states, with Africa providing some of the striking cases – Mauritius and Botswana. A number of writers working on Africa have thus expressed doubts about the wisdom of insisting on democracy and have counselled the implementation of variants of authoritarian regimes because Africa is not (yet) fit for democracy. This is not new. Literature on development and democracy has always posed the question about the fitness of poor countries for development. However as Amartya Sen (1999a) suggested, this is the wrong question: "A country does not have to be deemed fit for democracy; rather, it has to become fit through democracy." This also suggests that the chosen development path must be fit for democracy. In the literature on Western welfare states, the democratic nature of the state is taken for granted. However, the challenge is that of building a democratic developmental state. Social policy plays an important role in this process by strengthening the capabilities of citizens to partake in public life and the democratic process by increasing social trust and by ensuring a modicum of equality that makes the universal franchise truly meaningful.

Industrialisation once again

One of the slogans of the struggle for independence was the "struggle for industrialisation". This led to a not-always-successful search for or implementation of industrial policy. During the era of adjustment, the expression "industrial policy" was taboo in policy circles, being associated with the putatively failed "import substitution strategies". In the "Asia Miracle" report, the World Bank (1993) was compelled to acknowledge that the miracle was not evidence of the wisdom of having no industrial policy but that it was in fact evidence that the state could play a catalytic role in the process of industrialisation whether or not such industrialisation was inward or outward looking. The Bank was, of course, careful not to use the phrase "industrial strategy". The admission that Asia has a state-led industrial policy was accompanied by the observation that Africans could not replicate the Asian model for a whole range of arguments. In more recent years, there has been a softening of the dogma and the perceptions of the capacity of Africans to pursue strategies of industrialisation. However, within Africa, the role of industrial policy needs to be examined thoroughly to identify the specificities of such policies given our diverse circumstances and the prevailing world economic order.

Africa's natural resources

Africa has natural resources that, if harnessed, can enhance its development potential. This potential has been obscured by a debate focussed on the "resource curse", which suggests that Africa's tragedy is that its ability to carry out any policies has been overwhelmed by the rents it has acquired from its mineral wealth. This has been referred to as a "resource curse" founded on a rather tendentious deployment of data. Nevertheless, if there has been a "resource curse", it has been the massive extraction of surplus of Africa's minerals by foreign interests. Many other parts of the world have addressed these problems with various forms of "resource nationalism", the most successful in this respect being Norway.

Human capital

Africa has substantial human resources and is moving towards a more favourable demographic structure that can facilitate higher economic growth if the population is educated and provided with opportunities for employment. Although we still lag behind in terms of education, Africa is more educated today than it was at independence and it has the fastest-growing university population. However, more needs to be to done to reverse the deleterious effects of the assault on higher education that took place under structural adjustment.

Collective Action on the Global Front

Many things that affect economies are decided upon through the global arrangement, in which Africa is extremely weak. It is also an order in which our central concern – that of development – receives little attention. Dani Rodrik has hinted at the key aspects of such globalisation:

> A development-friendly international trading regime is one that does much more than enhance poor countries' access to markets in the advanced industrial countries. It is one that enables poor countries to experiment with institutional arrangements and leaves room for them to devise their own, possibly divergent, solutions to the developmental bottlenecks that they face. It is one that evaluates the demands of institutional reform not from the perspective of integration "what do countries need to do to integrate?" but from the perspective of development "what do countries need to do to achieve broad-based, equitable economic growth?" (Rodrik, 2001: 2).

This was related to an international order that denied poor countries the possibilities of industrialisation. Today, we are faced with an order that denies developing countries many of the instruments that were used by today's developed countries for their own industrialisation. We have to continue to fight for a global order that permits industrialisation through high levels of absorption of goods from developing countries and by allowing developing countries more policy space. We obviously must radically renegotiate the terms of our engagement with the rest of the world. Already some are defining our future role as a source of cheap labour, raw materials, etc., which has very much been Africa's situation for more than half a millennium.

Such renegotiation will demand greater pan-African cooperation and coordination of efforts.

CONCLUSION

We are often urged not to dwell too much on the past and instead to look to the future. But any strategy for the future must start from the initial conditions created by the maladjustment discussed above. A proper diagnosis must have this as its point of departure. More specifically, we have to respond to the question: What have been the cumulative effects of these errors and how do we address them? We have outlined some of the errors of commission and omission that have a bearing on our economies and that in many cases have undermined our capacity to exploit favourable international contexts, technological change, and immense natural resources.

African economies are generally recovering and growing fairly rapidly. One obvious problem is that a number of drivers behind the recovery were one-off events and are unlikely to be repeated in the immediate future. The challenge is to identify the internal drivers that can sustain the growth rates beyond the current era. These will include improved and prudent resource mobilisation and the use of Africa's vast resources through increased technological mastery and socially inclusive (and therefore politically sustainable) growth; we will turn to some of these issues in the next two lectures.

LECTURE 2
SOCIAL EQUALITY AND DEVELOPMENT

INTRODUCTION

There are many tasks that countries seeking to catch up economically must carry out in other spheres of their political economy. I have chosen to talk about two factors that are closely related. The first of these is social equality and the second is education. In today's lecture, I will focus on equality. The issue of social equality is a vast one, often involving weighty philosophical and moral considerations. I will confine myself to the narrow issue of economic development and social equality. Amartya Sen has usefully reminded us that "development is freedom" and social justice is not only a basic constituent of development in itself but is also an important instrument for its achievement (Sen, 1999b). I will therefore discuss development and social equality both as a means and as an end. However, I will also stress that social equality is not merely a technocratic matter as some are wont to make it, but an issue of political economy of the highest order.

In the context of rapid change, social policy has the instrumental value of embedding the development process within the wider society and legitimising the process of change itself. Economic development is an extremely dislocative process generating what the Germans called the "social question", which encompasses the process of social displacement that urbanisation entails, the production of "winners and losers", the dispossession of many, social anomie, etc. These must be expressly addressed if the whole process of accumulation and structural change is not to grind to a halt. Karl Polanyi argued that self-regulating markets "could not exist for any length of time without annihilating the human and natural substance of society" (Polanyi, 1946: 3). "For a century the dynamics of modern society were governed by a double movement: the market expanded continuously but this movement was met by a counter-movement checking the expansion in definite directions" (Polanyi, 1946: 130). Polanyi observed that historically society has reacted to defend itself against the ravages of the market and sought to "embed" the markets in social relations. Various forms of social policies were introduced to address the "social question" that the new economic transformations had posed and indeed it was during this era that the Bismarckian welfare state emerged in Germany. Social policies were introduced to address four basic challenges: the first and single most important one was to ensure the reproduction of society threatened by the new diseases that accompanied urbanisation and congested housing, hence the special, albeit patriarchal, attention to the family and the male breadwinner. The second was enhancing citizens' capabilities as key players in economic production and in the alleviation of poverty through education and training. The third was to provide citizens with the wherewithal to respond to the exigencies of change through the provision of workplace accident insurance and pensions in old age. The final challenge was to ensure redistribution and to guarantee an equitable process of change. Each of these tasks (reproduction, protection, production, and redistribution) was a constitutive element of the varieties of welfare states that emerged in different parts of the world and given the synergies among them they should be discussed simultaneously. However, for reasons of time and space, in this lecture I will focus only on the issue of distribution and development.

The question of social equality has been on the agenda throughout the history of mankind. In Africa, modern expressions of social equality took various forms of resistance against slavery and colonisation and were to constitute the leitmotif of the struggles for political liberation in Africa. Decolonisation was thus seen as the *sine qua non* for addressing poverty as the emblematic reminder of the presence of social injustice at the international and national levels. Nkrumah's call, to seek political freedom and the rest shall follow, was the iconic formulation of this understanding, suggesting that only with independence would African countries begin to address the many social questions, including those of glaring racial inequality, unequal regional development, and the incipient class differentiation spawned, albeit begrudgingly, by the colonial order. Many movements claimed attachment to a wide range of idiosyncratic socialist and populist ideologies that promised social equality. The manifestos of the nationalist movements were replete with promises of unity, economic development, and social equality (Mkandawire, 2009, 1999). In the event, political freedom in the form of national sovereignty was attained, but, as Chinua Achebe observed, the "rest" did not usually follow and in most cases new forms of social injustice, now driven by class, ethnicity, and gender, reared their head on the morrow of independence. What went wrong with the promise of social equality and development? I will argue that the interplay of ideas, interests, and structural conditions within and outside African nations have conspired to set aside the issue of equality and to produce the current condition of poor economic performance, social injustice, and political disempowerment of the majority of African people.

The focus on the national question[5]

The first factor behind the setting aside of the question of social equality was the "nation-building" argument, especially persuasive in the new states in Africa. A large part of the last century was spent resolving the "national question", which for much of Africa meant the end of colonial rule and the racial privilege injustice and constructing new nation states. Upon attaining independence, the nationalists in power simply refused to consider that these sovereign states might produce, perpetuate, or even deepen the class divisions, often by asserting that African culture was based on egalitarian communalism. Various particularistic ideologies, such as African socialism, Ujamaa, and African humanism, were advanced to codify such traditions. Other nationalists proclaimed adhesion to putatively progressive ideologies: Marxist-Leninism, Nkrumahism, etc. Nationalism demanded that the socialism pushed by Africans be, in some sense, "African".

There was, however, one immediate threat to the egalitarian aspirations that arose from the process of correcting historical injustices – deracialisation and indigenisation of key positions of privilege and power. These processes became a major aspect of national construction, in turn leading to very rapid growth in inequality among Africans themselves. Albert Hirschman provided an explanation for why in the early years of development high levels of inequality may be tolerated by society in that the upward movements of members of one's community suggest that soon it will be one's own turn. Albert Hirschman and Rothschild (1973) termed this the "tunnel effect". To the extent that the ascension of a member of one's community meant replacement of colonial privilege, it was hailed as "Africanisation" and the implied disparities were discounted. The "first national engineer" or the "first national millionaire" on the path chosen to address inequality

5 This section draws on Mkandawire (2009a).

were hailed as symbols of national achievement. A more recent version of this phenomenon is "Black Empowerment" in South Africa, which for a while at least seems to have received widespread approval among the black population. However, Hirschman warned that the passage of time tends to devalue the currency of this "effect". Eventually, the sense of relative deprivation steps in and raises questions about the post-colonial social dispensation. The "national question", which may have focussed on inter-national injustice and favoured the tunnel effect, is then faced with a "social question" that is focussed on intra-national social equality. In many cases, while it could be argued that addressing the "national injustice" had to precede addressing the "social injustice", there was no assurance that the sequence from the "national question" to the "social question" would be followed through. Indeed, we have sufficient evidence that many otherwise progressive social movements failed to follow through their social agenda.

The linear view

The second factor behind the setting aside of considerations of social equality and rights in the debate on development was a linear view of history, that posited the Western countries as the end point of history. In this view, the developed countries' welfare states and the social equality associated with them could only occur at much higher levels of development than those attained by today's less developed countries.

The high correlation of levels of economic development with the enjoyment of a number of social and political rights was construed to mean that poor countries would have to pass through a vale of tears of inequality and political repression before they could fully enjoy these rights. Two arguments were often advanced for this proposition. One was the functional necessity of the welfare state in the advanced countries where traditional forms of protection no longer existed. The "logic of industrialism" suggested that all countries were bound to move in the same direction because as industrialisation proceeded it inevitably led to demographic shifts, dislocation, and the erosion of some of the traditional forms of social provision – especially the family and community, necessitating some kind of welfare. The other was the question of affordability, which pointed to the high cost of the welfare state and the idea that this would be too costly for poor countries. A country would have to reach a certain income threshold before the state had high enough revenue to provide for the social service or to make the claims of social rights justiciable. There was also no point in insisting on distribution when there was nothing to distribute. The culinary expression was that one had first to enlarge the cake before one could have meaningful distribution.

On both these grounds, functional necessity and economic feasibility, comprehensive social policy was treated as something to be engaged in only after reaching a certain development threshold. All this was given an empirical gloss by Kuznets's work, which provided evidence suggesting that income distribution would become worse before it became better, producing the famous inverted U-curve that supported the Kuznets hypothesis (Kuznets, 1955).

This linear view is not borne out by history. First, many welfare policies in Europe were introduced at levels of per capita income that are comparable to or even lower than the per capita incomes of some of today's developing countries. Second, Kuznets's hypothesis has been subjected to quite a number of econometric analyses with better data sets and more robust economic tests and found to be empirically wanting. Countries have reached levels of equality in incomes at different levels of development and by following wildly different paths, some egalitarian and some not.

The developmentalist imperative

The third and most formidable factor militating against placing social equality at the core of development was the framing of the development agenda itself. For many years, an implicit and at times quite explicit view of the relationship between development and social equality was that it involved a trade-off or sequencing that excluded the simultaneous occurrence of equity and economic growth. The first argument is the classical one, which argues in favour of transferring economic surplus to those likely to invest rather than consume it – the productive rich – leaving out landlords and other groups living off unearned income. This was the view held by classical economists, Marxists, and neo-Keynesians, who all focussed their attention on functional income distribution, which involved the distribution of incomes – wages, profits, and rents – among "factors of production" (labour, capital, and land) or to different social groups (workers, capitalists, and landowners); we will return to this thesis later.

Additionally, in line with this understanding for much of the 1960s and 1970s, "growth-first" and trickle-down views permeated a good deal of the thinking about policy. This was a period of rapid growth, and one can thus understand some of the hopes that growth would suffice not to deal with problems of distribution.

We should also recall that this was a period of industrialisation through import substitutions and explicit industrial policy. This often created highly organised labour in large-scale, oligopolistic firms, able to bargain for a share of the profits and rents earned by the oligopolies, often generating a "wage-technique" spiral, in which the capitalists sought higher productivity by adopting capital-intensive techniques, which, in return, provoked demands from labour for a higher share of the earnings (Arrighi, 1973). In the worst case, this led to what Peter Evans termed "an anti-Schumpeterian triangle" of state, labour, and capital "where protected workers, protected entrepreneurs and the state elites and employees engaged in rentier games, driven by a political logic rather than by the driving force of competition and innovating" (Figueira, 2007).

Thus, although social policy was couched in the language of universalism, the economic models associated with it and the structural changes it engendered inevitably led to highly segmented welfare regimes. Workers in the large-scale formal sector and in government often enjoyed high levels of protection, while the majority of the labour force was employed under extremely insecure and often highly exploitative conditions.

The basic needs era and growth with equity

The consequences of all this became obvious by the end of the 1970s, when it was realised that growth was accompanied by poverty and inequity and that in the absence of deliberate policies to shape the patterns of growth, there was no guarantee that growth would trickle down in amounts sufficient to begin to address poverty, let alone equity. Consequently, a new generation of strategies aimed at meeting basic human needs or inducing "growth with equity" was proposed by the ILO (1972) and the World Bank (Chenery *et al.*, 1974), respectively. These strategies were short-lived, however, their demise being linked to the economic crisis of the 1970s and the ideological ascendancy of neoliberalism in leading developed countries and international financial institutions. Many developing countries had to turn to Bretton Wood Institutions (BWIs) for financial support, where they were confronted with pristine neoclassical stylisation of economies. However, even in its brief heyday, the basic needs strategy attracted considerable scepticism from some important quarters of the development establishment, so it was never given much of a chance, especially with respect to its call for equity.

THE ADJUSTMENT YEARS: SOCIALLY BLIND MACROECONOMICS

The first victim of Structural Adjustment Programs was the claims by states that they would intervene in the economy to ensure not only economic performance but also certain social outcomes, such as equity and poverty alleviation. The segmented "welfare states" that post-colonial regimes had instituted became a target of both ideological and fiscal attack. On the ideological plane, whatever gains had been accrued to the workers in the formal sector were now seen as "distortions" in labour markets brought about by the activities of rent-seeking urban coalitions. Social expenditures were seen as straining the fiscus and as a source of financial instability. The disappearance of poverty from the policy agenda was accompanied by the disappearance of "development" as something that state policies deliberately pursued beyond simply overseeing the spontaneous market processes. Earlier "developmentalist" arguments for social policy as one of the key objectives and instruments of development simply disappeared. "Adjustment" to the exigencies of a putatively highly competitive world market became the key word. The view that there was indeed a conflict between good economic policies and social equality, which had been challenged by the "growth with equity" literature, regained ascendancy during the 1980s, following the "oil crisis" of the 1970s and the stagflation in the advanced economies. The commitment of states to the provision of protection to the citizens and the need for wealth redistribution were severely put to the test by the new economic regime, which sought to dismantle the institutional arrangements that had sought to embed the market in a social order that was equitable and protected citizens from the "blind compulsions" of the market. In the developing countries, economic development ceased to be something that suggested intentionality and that called for a strategic alignment of means and ends. Instead, it was to be the outcome of the interplay and whims of "market forces". As for the old socialist world, the collapse of the planned economies and authoritarian regimes undermined the egalitarian policies they had pursued in the social sphere. Nationalist ideologies were dismissed as self-serving obfuscations that had been used by those in power to fool their fellow citizens. In the neoliberal world, community is at best the unintended consequence of individuals' pursuit of self-interest and not something that reflects commonality of goals. The memorable expression of this view was Mrs Thatcher's assertion that "There is no such thing as community", thus circumventing the old biblical question: "Am I my brother's keeper?" The new doctrine of greed, by dismissing grievances from among the factors behind conflict, simply made nonsense of notions of equity and solidarity as cohesive elements. For the neoliberals, the workings of the free market ensured social equality of opportunities. It allowed free choice of individuals and it ensured that everyone was paid according to their due as measured by the marginal productivity of the asset they brought to the market. The only injustice recognised was that of anyone earning "rents" generated by "distortions" of the market. Although there was a vast literature demonstrating that such "distortions" were inherent to the real existing markets because of information imperfections, economies of scale, and other structural rigidities, the dominant view was exclusively focussed on state-induced distortions. Even when it was admitted that the market outcomes may be unjust, there was always the presumption that the social injustice caused by the state's intervention to correct "market failures" was somehow more abhorrent than that due to omission and neglect by the market.

As for political rights, it was simply asserted that the liberalisation of the economy is the *sine qua non* of the liberation of polity. This then subjugated democracy to the immediate economic imperatives of the market. The triumph of neoliberalism was such that democracies were judged not by the criteria of social equality but by how well they would carry out the neoliberal project. Any notion of redistribution had to pass the test of "incentive compatibility" as defined by neoliberalism. Would the redistribution blunt the incentives for accumulation by the capitalists of exertion by workers? The presumption was always, as observed by Latin Americans, that the rich were not investing enough because they were not rich enough while the poor were not exerting themselves enough because they were not poor enough. To deal with the conundrum, measures were introduced to shift the distribution of income towards the rich. The rich should be encouraged to invest while the poor should exercise their patience and exert themselves more until the cake was large enough to share. This involved not only tax exemptions to improve the "investment climate" but also often weakened social protection measures that were seen as "distorting the market" and serving as disincentives for hard work.

It was generally understood that these shifts in income distribution would cause social protest. It was therefore necessary to have regimes that could act unencumbered by concerns for social rights. It then became a matter of faith that the "invisible hand" needed the protection of highly visible jackboots. Pinochet was to be the iconic symbol of jackboots at the service of the invisible hand and many little Pinochets were promoted in the rest of the world. The preference for such regimes remained an open secret, and within Africa, the jackbooted "strong adjusters", such as Museveni and Rawlings, were held up as the "new leaders" of the continent.

The consequences of SAP were severe. Deindustrialisation, retrenchment of the state, and devaluation had devastating impacts, especially on the urban population, often leading to the pauperisation of the middle classes. This immediately led to greater economic differentiation, which in turn led to increased urban crime and the rise of the "gated communities" in African cities. As a consequence of the withdrawal of the state from the provision of public goods to rural areas and the withdrawal of state marketing boards from areas where the private sector was unwilling to bear the costs of servicing, this led to further marginalisation of more remote areas.

The hardships imposed on the urban population were couched in the language of equality. The new regime was said to be finally addressing the "urban bias" that had generated the rural-urban divide and was pulling the rag from under the feet of protected labour. In the event, what the new policies achieved was simply to shift poverty from the rural to the urban areas. The bridging of the gap between the rural and the urban populations was achieved not by improving the productivity or access to welfare of the former but by pressing down the living conditions of the latter.

Table 2.1: GINI coefficients in the 1990s

Country name	Gini
Namibia	74
Zimbabwe	73
Lesotho	61
Central African Republic	60
South Africa	59
Zambia	56
Mali	55
Swaziland	55
Kenya	54
Cameroon	51
Malawi	50
Nigeria	50
Senegal	50
Botswana	49
Guinea	49
Madagascar	48
Tanzania	48
Somalia	47
Mauritania	46
Niger	46
Rwanda	45
Uganda	45
Gabon	44
Djibouti	43
Ethiopia	43
Mozambique	43
Ghana	40
Sierra Leone	39
Mauritius	38
Benin	37

Source: UNWIDER Database

POST-WASHINGTON CONSENSUS

Growing inequality and poverty threatened the entire edifice over which the "invisible hand" reigned and in some places fanned violent conflict. The structural adjustment that was supposed to ensure the reign of the invisible hand generated so many social problems that it was felt that it must be given a "human face" by attaching to it programmes to mitigate its social effects. Bilateral and multilateral donors set aside significant volumes of funds aimed at "mitigating" the "social dimensions of adjustment". Such social policy was essentially ameliorative and designed to smooth the rough edges of structural adjustment. It was also to give political legitimacy to the economic policies. Many of the seemingly progressive ideas were intended to shore up a beleaguered economic model. Therefore, while the thinking about policies and social policy changed substantially, these new initiatives were still tethered to an economic model that severely restricted their reach, were poorly funded, and were marginal to the core socio-economic regime. Furthermore, they completely avoided the issue of equity.

The new turn to equity

In 2006, the World Bank devoted its flagship *World Development Report* to the issue of equity (World Bank, 2006). The report was hailed as a major breakthrough. It underscored the thesis that there were always hard choices, but that in fact there were no iron laws that bound society to injustice until countries had reached some mystical threshold before addressing the issues of social equality. As is always the case, there was an academic counterpart to these changes, generating theoretical and empirical evidence showing that the reduction of inequality was good for development. Several arguments were advanced. First, with better data it was easy to disprove the Kuznets thesis and the "equity/growth" trade-offs. First, in the African case, the opposite of Kuznets occurred. Countries with highly unequal economies were left behind by colonial racial hierarchies. During the first decade, there were significant declines in inequality. These were to be reversed by structural adjustment, with African inequality moving closer to the notorious Latin American one even as countries such as Brazil reduced theirs. Second, it was argued that inequality was in fact bad for growth and that, instead, equality may be an important stimulus to growth through various channels – human capital formation, political stability, market size, overall macroeconomic policy, etc. The question then was identifying development paths that ensured the virtuous cycles of increasing equality and growth.

The challenge of capitalist growth and equality

There were three aspects of the new bow towards equity. The first concerned the definitions of equity. The disagreement was not over the normative value of equity *per se* but, as Amartya Sen argued, over "equality of what". Economists distinguish between two measures of income distribution – functional and personal income distribution.

In the context of economic development, the central question was about the generation and allocation of economic surplus. The ideal was to allocate surplus to the social groups likely to invest. The classical view was that distribution is not only a final outcome, but in fact plays a central role in determining other aspects of economic performance. Classical economies favoured the transfer of surplus to profit-earners rather than to rents and wages.

It is thus not surprising that Arthur Lewis could state:

> the central fact of economic development is that the distribution of incomes is altered in favour of the saving class. The major source of savings are profits, and if we find that savings are increasing as a proportion of national income, we may take it for granted that this is because the share of profits in the national income is increasing. (Lewis, 1954: 157).

The debate on inequality evolved around personal income distribution, which overthrew the classical and neo-Keynesian preoccupation with functional income distribution. The preference for the focus on personal income distribution rather than functional income distribution had both practical and ideological underpinnings. On the ideological level, the new framing of the income distribution was basically institution-neutral because it used a measure of income distribution that did not indicate the mode of production. This is in sharp contrast to both the classical and the neo-Keynesian focus, which quite consciously dealt with capitalist economies, with its differentiated and class-based sources of income

The second aspect is that equality was actually confined to that of opportunities and not of outcomes. The mantra was that of providing a "level playing field", completely ignoring other social factors that would unevenly affect the incidence of these opportunities.

The third is that the equality that was referred to was the "initial" one and not the one that was produced contemporaneously with the development process. Most of the regressions used to support the thesis were based on past reductions of inequality. Land reform in the past would have an impact on growth today. The real political economy was the contemporaneous distributive impact of current policies. The model of adjustment was actually premised on uneven development as the process proceeded. The new agenda on equality was still tethered or subservient to economic policy that ensured its reproduction if not magnification (Garuda, 2000). As the advocates of new equality based on personal income distribution recognised the capitalist nature of the economies in question, the issue of the "incentive compatibility" of the redistributive measures arose. Thus, no sooner had these institutions pronounced their commitment to equity, these advocates began to backpedal on their insistence on its importance. World Bank officials actually began to downplay the equity issue because they considered the "transitional costs" of moving from a high inequality growth path such as the one they had mapped out for Africa to a more equitable one to be too high. After arguing that the distribution of wealth rather than current income was more efficacious, the then Chief Economist of the World Bank argued:

> The arguments summarized above tend to suggest that redistribution of "wealth" from rich to less-rich people may have a positive impact on growth ... In order to be efficient and growth-enhancing, redistribution should be concerned with wealth rather than current income or consumption expenditures. It is doubtful that such direct wealth redistribution is feasible or without cost. Redistributing property can only be done under exceptional circumstances, which often involve political violence, and can hardly be considered economic policy options. Land reform is a case in point (Bourguignon, 2004).

Therefore, at the end of the day, equity even of personal income distribution was out. What was demanded was the eradication of absolute poverty and not inequality. It was argued that with inequality untouched, economic growth would be good for the poor. In the Millenium Development Goals, only one of the goals explicitly addressed inequality by suggesting that efforts should be made to increase the share of the poorest quintile. Subsequent reviews of the progress that was being made hardly mentioned this goal.

Back to the classics

Ideological obfuscation notwithstanding, the problem of functional income distribution has reappeared. Even the IMF has suggested that the following share of wages in the GDP may have contributed to the "subprime" financial crisis. The focus on functional distribution helps one to understand the recent economic growth and some of the "social pacts" that have managed the tension between the exigencies of accumulation and those of equity. The benefits of unequal income distribution in terms of functional distribution are conditional, first and foremost, upon the reinvestment by capitalists of the incomes accruing to them or the ability of the state to tax and reinvest some of the tax revenue. The real problem in development has been designing socio-political arrangements that ensure both "patient capital" and "patient labour" to underpin their accumulation and innovation systems. That is the context of catching up: patient labour in the labour market should have as a counterpart patient capital in the financial market. For example, workers should be "patient" enough to accept a lower wage on the assumption that higher profits will lead to higher investment and, therefore, employment and higher wages in the future. A critical assumption in this is that capitalist systems would have high levels of reinvestment of profits. However, there is the problem of credible commitments against opportunism when employers retrench labour through the acquisition of even more capital-intensive technologies.

Let us start with the East Asian "miracle" economies. The literature on these economies stresses that these economies have had low levels of inequality as measured by the GINI coefficient. However, this is only a partial view of inequality in these countries. It relates only to personal income distribution. The true picture of the Korean experience, for instance, is that there is (a) inequality in functional distribution of income in favour of profits and (b) a high level of equity in terms of personal income distribution. You (1998) provided evidence that the share of wages in all the high-performance East Asian economies, except Hong Kong, fell below the average of the relevant income group. Low inequality as measured by the GINI coefficient and high profit shares coexisted primarily due to the unusually even distribution of wages. This is apparently a general phenomenon with profound political economic implications. Daudey and Garcia-Peñalosa (2007) argued:

the share of wages in all the high performance East Asian economies, except Hong Kong were favourable to capital and increased its return. Our results imply that policies that raise the share of capital have a substantial cost in terms of inequality. This means not only that governments should carefully assess the desirability of such policies, but also that external shocks that tend to reduce the labour share may call for corrective policies in order to offset their distributional implications (Daudey and García-Peñalosa, 2007).

The success of the East Asian models was thus due to a reconciliation: on the one hand, high inequality in terms of functional income distribution caused by policies to ensure profit while suppressing financial and land rents and, on the other hand, achievement of high personal income distribution by initial land reform and wage compression. The high growth rate was ensured by high reinvestment of profit, which generated high levels of employment and in a way legitimised the skewed functional income distribution.

The political economy of redistribution and growth

We have suggested that the "logic" of the East Asian model involved investment–profit–investment (Akyüz, 1996), which kept the wage share low but managed to achieve equitable personal income distribution through wage compression. An important lesson here is that these models require "patient capital" and "patient labour". Any decision to restrict wages in favour of profits must be accompanied by measures that ensure that the resulting profits will be productively invested. Indeed, this is one of the more difficult challenges of social policy and is at the core of any normative justification for favouring profit in the functional distribution of income.[6]

How were labour and capital made patient? These economies were authoritarian: the state "delivered" cheap labour to capital and state repression played a central role in keeping wages growing at a rate lower than the productivity and, therefore, profits. Direct repression of labour had been too frequent a feature of many "catch-up" strategies. There is

---

6. Paul Samuelsson once defined exploitation as the share of capitalist consumption to total profit. A situation in which capitalists invested all their profits was therefore not deemed to be exploitation.

a vast amount of literature on the features of the Eastern developmental states that needs little elaboration (Castells, 1992, Deyo, 1989, Leftwich, 1994)

This repression was generally justified in the literature by those who argued against "premature" unionisation or any other workers' rights or extension of social rights in the name of development. Amartya Sen (2003) gave this view the acronym BLAST (for "blood, sweat, and tears"), which was at times attributed to the protestant ethic of Weber or evoked by leaders as the necessary sacrifices for the nation or a socialist future.

One of the problems faced by many developing countries is related to the failure to ensure the profitable investment of accumulated funds and to reduce the misuse of surplus. Vast amounts of money have been lost through conspicuous consumption. The shopping mall rather than the factory is the symbol of the new African city. The East Asian model has been characterised by high levels of investment. What made capitalists reinvest by translating high profits into high savings and high business? The answer to the question is the heart of the "developmental state" literature. A number of arguments have been advanced in the development state literature, which have included the nationalism of the bourgeoisie, the close collaboration between the state and business ("embeddedness" of the developmental state), the coercive force of the state and its ability through carrots and sticks to make the business class buy into its project, and the autonomy to force capitalists to invest (Koo and Kim, 1992)[7]. On the reinvestment of surplus, the instruments included "severe restrictions on luxury consumption, both directly through restricting the import and domestic production of luxury consumption goods, and indirectly through high taxation and restrictions on consumer credits, although the mix of measures differed across countries"(Akyüz et al., 1998). The other measures were restriction of earnings from the financial sector. This was achieved by the state controlling or owning the banks, elimination of speculative investment opportunities, and restrictions on the outflow of capital. If we add to these the land reform measures that

---

7   Park Chung Hee's junta arrested leading businesspersons on charges of "illicit wealth accumulation" during previous regimes, with full intention to punish. Very soon, however, Park turned around, completely pardoning those arrested in exchange for economic co-operation. He asked them to participate in his ambitious industrialization projects as leading entrepreneurs, and subsequently allocated to them the bulk of foreign and domestic capital along with many other trade and tax privileges" (Koo and Kim, 1992: 125).

basically eliminated rents for landlords, we have an economy in which profit reigned supreme.

Many African countries are striving to consolidate their democracy and the authoritarian path of ensuring high growth and greater equity is not, and hopefully will not be, open to them. The challenge then is to find functionally equivalent arrangements for attaining those objectives within a democratic framework. Many countries allocate limited amounts of their budgets to social expendititure. The argument in support of these low levels of expenditure is that of affordability and the putative trade between growth and welfare However, the co-existence of the developmental states and more extensive social policy in other parts of the world or among other latecomers (e.g. Mauritius) may suggest that the low levels of redistributive expenditure or taxation is not a reflection of ineluctable exigencies of accumulation but a reflection of political choices made.

The Nordic model has structurally similar features to the one outlined above for the developmental states but is based on entirely normative and political economy premises. Nordic countries were characterised not so much by a high share of wages in the GDP but by wage compression. They too were high-profit–high-investment economies with high levels of equity as measured by personal income distribution. Moene and Wallenstein (2003) formalised this model into a "social democratic development model". Workers adopt a "patient stance" by accepting wage increases that are lower than labour productivity as long as the profits are reinvested to create more and better-paying jobs. It is "wage compression" that accounts for much of the equality in welfare states and not the share of wages in the GDP. Wage compression was not always used for egalitarian purposes. The need for it can arise for a whole range of reasons, including efficiency and management of labour relations, and it has been used under various political regimes for different political reasons. In social democracies, it has been used as a tool for equity ("equal pay for equal work") but also as an instrument for promoting efficacy by restructuring the economy towards more profitable activities. The wage compression pushes out less efficient producers and favours high-productivity firms.

However, the Nordic social compacts were founded on a political order that was fundamentally democratic; various social interests were given room to organise themselves and to articulate their interests freely. This model is fundamentally reformist within a capitalist economy and so has certain prerequisites in which regulations held down market segmentation and wage dispersion (minimum wages, industry-wide wage agreements, etc.). The first of these is the ideology and shared developmental vision. The ideologies for reducing inequality have drawn on nationalism, notions of fairness, justice, and solidarity that are anathema to the individualistic ethos of the neoliberal era. This organisational capacity of partners and their political inclusion has been conducive to producing what has been referred to as "democratic developmental welfare states" underpinned by social compacts.

Economic growth (and full employment) is important in both sustaining and legitimising such social arrangements. Indeed, beside the intrinsic value of such social arrangements, they have proved efficacy in resolving the conundrum of "patient capital" and "patient labour" or of attaining a modicum of social inclusion and equality in what are fundamentally capitalist systems with their inherent disequalising dynamics. Such arrangements have lent greater flexibility to the system by ensuring workers social protection against the vagaries of the market.

The compacts only make sense if they involve negotiation over substantive issues. The kinds of "participation" (of the PRSP kind) that accompanied structural adjustment were usually merely a charade and were excluded from discussions of the core economic adjustment policies. They were also designed to keep away organisations representing those directly engaged in production, such as labour unions. The state plays an important role in such compacts. Social compacts are not a self-sustaining equilibrium. They often need an external actor to provide the framework for negotiations and to ensure respect by all parties for the conditions of the bargain. The predispositions of the state towards various actors can facilitate social pacts. The state can help by providing a credible societal vision and by coordinating expectations of different social constituencies.

Where are we now?

Obviously, the experience of the Nordic countries is subject to path dependence and context specificity and each county will have to devise its own political and institutional arrangements. In the African case, Mauritius has been cited as approaching this. The Nordic model flourished during the era of "embedded liberalism" when individual states enjoyed greater policy space. In the era of liberalisation, labour market regulation has been relaxed or removed, so much of the growing inequality is driven by both the declining share of wages in the national income and the decompression of wages as the skilled labour, especially that in the "globalised" part of the labour market, is paid much more than labour in the less formal markets. However, even in the era of globalisation, the Nordic model has performed well and most spectacularly in Finland.

The news from Africa is nowadays generally positive. We are witnessing steady consolidation of democratic governance. In many countries, economies are growing. In the earlier days of the new African democracies, economic policy tended to be orthodox, with some leaders equating political liberalisation with economic liberalism. Many of the new democracies did not pay much attention to issues of equality. With the passage of time, the politics of democracy tended to push towards more heterodox responses (Mkandawire, 2004).

The central message is that the issue of social equality can be embedded in a broader context of social policy and democratic governance. We must imagine social arrangements that will bring labour and other actors directly engaged in the productive process into "social compacts" that can drive the process of economic development in an equitable and democratic way.

LECTURE 3

BRINGING THE UNIVERSITIES BACK IN

The choice of the title is deliberate. It is intended to suggest reversing the process of marginalisation of knowledge generated by African universities from sites where fundamental decisions on the future of Africa are made. It also aims to suggest that any meaningful future for Africa must be organically linked to the intellectual, scientific, and technological capacities and endeavours of its institutions of higher learning. By universities, I mean not only the activities within the universities, but the entire infrastructure that sustains the intellectual life of institutions of learning – publication, libraries, research centres, and networks.

In my inaugural lecture at the London School of Economics (Mkandawire, 2010), I used as a title Mwalimu Nyerere's statement that "Africa Must Run While Others Walk". This lecture is given in the same spirit.

I would like to preface my argument for "bringing the universities back in" with three assumptions: (a) that we agree that Africa lags behind badly in terms of a wide range of social indicators and that lagging behind has huge implications; (b) that, as is implicit in Mwalimu Nyerere's remarks, Africa must run fast to "catch up"; and (c) that in this process of addressing the question of "catching up", education will play an important role. I would like to stress at the outset that my notion of "catching up" refers to material and technological conditions.

The first point regarding catching up is its intentionality. "Catching up" involves the intention of key social actors to move the economy at a faster pace than would be possible under the spontaneous functioning of the market. This intentionality is informed by a wide range of issues, including ideologies, a sense of political and even military vulnerability, and a sense of humiliation entailed by "backwardness" and the human trait of emulation. It is, in other words, a highly political phenomenon often encapsulated in various ideologies of "developmentalism" and "modernisation".

Those of a more linear disposition towards history argue that countries must go through various stages and each of these states has certain prerequisites. This view spawned Rostow's "stages of growth" theory of development (Rostow, 1960). However, in his seminal work, Alexander

Gerschenkron (1962) challenged this view by pointing out that while in a general sense the less advanced countries would be said to follow the general path traced by the "pioneers", in a fundamental sense the actual path taken by the followers would be different. In this nonlinear view, the path to be followed by the "latecomers" need not slavishly follow that of the pioneers for several reasons. First, the actual nature and attributes of the backwardness of the followers would not be exactly the same as those of the forerunners at the same level of development. For one, the existence of countries that had already traversed the particular path would have changed the "initial conditions" for the latecomers. As a consequence, the followers would have at their disposal knowledge and lessons that were not available to the forerunners and, therefore, the path followed would be based on the "advantage of backwardness" that was derived from the exploitation of the knowledge and experience of the forerunners. However, Alexander Gerschenkron insisted that "catching up" is anything but linear. The past of the forerunners does not intellectually map out the path that the followers must slavishly and teleologically follow. In the words of Albert Hirschman (1981), they do not have to "perform like wind-up toys and to lumber through the various stages of development single-mindedly". There would be no point in investing so much in the study of history if it involved simply regurgitating scripts that countries must follow. The "late" comers will need to study the paths traversed by others in order to determine the optimal sequencing appropriate to their conditions and to learn how to avoid the errors of the past. For the "late, late, late comers of Africa", the experience to look at is not only that of the front runners but that of virtually every development in every part of the world. In this respect, our poor knowledge of Asia and its spectacular economic performance points to a serious lacuna in our knowledge that needs to be addressed by a course on Asia in our university curriculum.

Economists have more recently taken up the implications of initial conditions and lagging behind. The simple view of "catching up" is premised on the notion that there is a negative relationship between the productivity growth at time t_n and the initial levels of income at time t_0. Countries that are technologically backward have the advantage of exploiting existing technologies and generating growth rates in productivity that are higher than those of the more advanced ones. Furthermore, the followers would be driven by an entirely different "spirit" or ideology, including, of course, the drive to "catch up", which was not meaningful for the forerunners.

Obviously, convergence does not happen automatically, as suggested in the more simplistic versions of convergence. The exploitation of this advantage is conditional upon what Moses Abramovitz (1995) referred to as "social capability", which includes not only the human capability to learn, adapt, and generate new ideas and ways of doing things, but also social cohesion, the cultural ability to tame or master technology and to give it cultural meaning relating to the new social changes, and the political institutions for handling the contradictions that social change raises. In the absence of such social capacity, countries will not be able to exploit the vast human knowledge and may indeed suffer from what Gunnar Myrdal (1957) referred to as the "backwash effects" caused by the negative effects of the economic growth of others. This nonlinear view of history and development immediately suggests the importance of learning from others so as not to simply retrace wastefully the path traversed by the forerunners, but learning with the purpose of not only of "leap-frogging" or moving through the various phases at greater speed than attained by the forerunners, but also of avoiding some of the errors they may have made over certain phases. This entails learning not only about ideas from abroad but also about one's capacities and weaknesses. Learning is not just about others but also about us. Perhaps in another sphere the proverbial injunction "Know Thyself" is important in the quest for "catching up", which involves leapfrogging. This in turn causes the catch-up mode of proceeding to be fraught with all kinds of risks. Great leaps forward have been made at great human cost, and the old adage "look before you leap" assumes even greater force in social matters. "Catching up" requires that countries know themselves and their own history, which has set the "initial conditions" for any future progress. They need a deep understanding of their culture not only for self-reaffirmation but in order to capture the strong points of their culture and institutions that will see their societies through rapid social change. We need to understand where we have been and where we have been taken. This would also allow our societies to make informed political and moral choices about the oath to take, the pace at which the journey will be carried out, and the incidence of the benefits and costs of this collective endeavour. The real issue about "catching up" is not that of simply taking on every wretched instrument used by the pioneers to achieve what they have – wars, slave labour, child labour, colonialism, Gulags, concentration camps – but finding more efficacious and morally acceptable ways of improving the life chances of millions of people. We should recall that many of the lessons that others only learn *ex post* come to us *ex ante*. Therefore, we do not have to make the same mistakes. We can leapfrog, invent new solutions, copy, etc.

In the manner of Gerschenkron, I have argued that in order to catch up, "late, late" comers will need to attain levels of education and learning that are far higher than those attained by the pioneers at similar levels of economic development. I have further argued that while earlier forms of "primitive accumulation" relied on brawn, the new ones will rely more on brains. Increases in productivity will drive the catching-up processes much more than the mobilisation of financial and human resources.[8] One explanation for the brutality of the development process is that nations were groping in the dark. Finally, I would also argue that this broader development agenda will call for much broader systems of education and knowledge than suggested by the simple "human capital" models or the "education for all" campaigns that focus only on primary school education. The learning required is not rote learning in which Africa still follows the routes traced by others. Rather, it involves creative, purposeful and strategic learning at all levels of the educational system.

Problems of learning

Learning from the past is, of course, not easy. One has to deal not only with the scientific processes of acquiring, disseminating, and accumulating knowledge but also with the current economic conditions and political exigencies and subjectivities that impinge on such an endeavour. However, beyond politics and subjectivities, we must recognise that there are other problems inherent in the learning process. Technology is not generously transferred but acquired through immense effort and against increasingly forbidding barriers.

---

8 This point is articulated by Abramovitz as follows:
Those who are behind, however, have the potential to make a larger leap. New capital can embody the frontier of knowledge, but the capital it replaces was technologically superannuated. So - the larger the technological and, therefore, the productivity gap between leader and follower, the stronger the follower's potential for growth in productivity; and, other things being equal, the faster one expects the follower's growth rate to be. Followers tend to catch up faster if they are initially more backward. (Abramovitz, 1986: 386-7).

Chasing a moving target
The first problem with "catching up" is that the latecomers are targeting a moving object. The advanced countries are not standing still but are in actual fact forging ahead and are also undergoing changes not only with respect to capacities but also in terms of aspirations and objectives. Others have observed, in a minatory manner, that the world will not wait for Africa to catch up. It is in this light that Nyerere's call for athletic prowess on behalf of Africans takes on a profound meaning.

Inability and unwillingness to share knowledge
The second problem is the ability and willingness of the leading countries to share their experiences and knowledge with others in any usable manner. In much of the debate about "technology transfer", there is the presumption that the more advanced countries will lower the ladder to facilitate the ascendancy of poor countries to higher levels of productivity. In neoclassical models, technology has, until recently, been described as an exogenous factor that is readily available on the "shelves" from which poor countries draw freely; this is the convergence thesis in its simplest form. However, the historical record is that access to technology has been anything but free and willingness to pay may not be enough. The pioneers may simply not be willing to share their knowledge for commercial or geopolitical reasons.

We should not forget that knowledge is not only power, but in our market-driven world, an asset, especially if its "public good" attributes are attenuated by such restrictions on access as intellectual property rights. Global debates and negotiations on such rights have clearly shown that the more advanced countries will fight to limit access to such knowledge. These restrictive practices are not new. "Latecomers" have always had to struggle openly or surreptitiously against the prevailing property regimes. Generally, the leading countries have sought to "kick away the ladder", to borrow from a book of the same title (Chang, 2002), by introducing a formidable arsenal of regulations and restrictions through intellectual property rights. To the extent that rents from property rights are a significant part of the exports of developed countries, we should expect an increase in constraints. In the days when some of the "late industrialisers" developed, the property rights regime was much less restrictive, often evoked when borrowed or stolen technologies were used to conquer markets abroad and not for domestic markets. The situation today is dramatically different. The restrictions apply even in cases in which the new technologies are used for the production of the domestic market (Chang, 2002)

Even if they are willing to share knowledge, the lead countries may not have any mechanisms for transmitting knowledge or repackaging it for developmental purposes, or may have been afflicted by collective amnesia that completely distorts their history, forgetting their failures and, in the opposite direction, vividly and selectively recollecting and idealising their successes. This mystification of the past may have progressed so far as to make the lessons irretrievable for contemporary use. The main culprit here is the temptation to lump together everything that happened simultaneously as inseparable or to assume that all the things we now deem good for development must have happened at the same time. The retrofitting and translation of the contingent into the functional gives a logical purpose to every policy pursued in the past and assigns to the policy makers of the time tasks and objectives of which they may never have been consciously aware. Indeed, the policies may never have been intended and may not have been necessary, but once adopted they were sufficient to account for some of the social outcomes of the development models. Once something from the past is given an *ex post* logical necessity, it is then impossible to see how anything else would have happened without it. We must also recall that even if we could establish that something may indeed have served a purpose at some historical point, we will not have established that there was nothing else that was functionally equivalent that would have worked. The point here is that many "lessons" that have been learned by the forerunners *ex post* are often presented misleadingly as evidence of the *ex ante* prescience and insightfulness of the leaders of the nations concerned. In light of all this, latecomers have to learn how to separate the wheat from the chaff and may have to carry out their own archaeological work to discover the really useful lessons buried under the rubble of distortions, mystification, and confusion.

Willingness to learn

The third constraint is the willingness of the "latecomers" to learn. Here, we face the fraught issues of intellectual openness, "cultural bias", and hegemonic pressures that direct eyes in one direction. In the case of Africa, our learning antennae have been directed towards the Western experience, and even within that they have been limited to that of our erstwhile colonial masters and the new hegemony. In addition, various expressions of chauvinism may persuade some that learning from others is demeaning, especially when some parts of the world have appropriated human knowledge for themselves. The arrogance of those who possess certain desirable forms of knowledge or skills may be a turn-off. One may recall here how the "Negritude movements" felt the need to respond to the West's claims of rationality as an exclusive trait of its culture by stressing emotion as the outstanding quality of black people.

In some of the debates about education, there is a misleading polarisation between transnationalisation and nationalisation. The former argues that knowledge is without borders and that African academics must join the global academy of scholarship or be left behind. The opposed thesis is that our institutions of learning must do away with their cultural dependence and extroversion and focus instead on the needs of their own societies. While the first view would encourage African universities to engage with the many forms of ranking of universities, the latter view suggests that African universities should focus not on abstract notions of "world class" standards but on being useful to their own societies, and in the words of Dr. Aggrey, "only the best is good enough for Africa". But universities have a dual function, of self-reflection and of opening the vast world of human knowledge. The founding fathers of independent Africa were quite remarkably conscious of the national and international roles of universities in enhancing the continent's own well-being and that of the comity of nations.

The capacity of the latecomers to learn

The fourth constraint is the capacity to learn. The issue here may simply be that of having no institutions of learning to learn critically and adapt the lessons with a view to "leapfrogging" over some of the phases. An important point about catching up is the acquisition of knowledge through local training and contact with centres of skills and knowledge abroad. In this process, the cross-border movement of people has played an important role.

The post-colonial experience

Education in post-colonial Africa has gone through three phases. The first one was dominated by nationalist and developmentalist views about education. The second consisted of the crisis and adjustment years in which attempts were made to subject the education systems to the laws of the market and to fiscal retrenchment. The third is the current one, characterised by an uneasy relationship between the education system and the economic recovery, vastly improved academic freedom with the retreat of the "Khakhicracy" and demise of one-party rule, and the ongoing re-evaluation of the dogmatic neoliberal assault on higher education.

The nationalist/developmentalist phase

In the early years of independence, the national universities were not only a symbol, together with national flags and anthems, of the birth of the new nation but were placed at the centre stage of the "Nationalist Project", which had political, cultural, and economic dimensions. Both cultural renaissance and economic development pointed to the need for universities. During the struggle for independence, nationalism sought historical and cultural anchors — or a usable past — for its sustenance. In the early years of independence, there was a genuine attempt to find new expressions for what was happening, or expected to be established, in post-colonial Africa. African intellectuals shared this quest.

The early nationalists were quite convinced that education and "manpower" or human capital were crucial to the nation-building project and developmental aspirations. Nation-building called for a trained cadre that would not only replace the thin layer of colonial officials that manned colonial administrations but would also extend both the size and the reach of the state to take on the much broader range of policies that were imposed on it by the exigencies of national development. "Indigenisation" or "Africanisation" programmes and national integration were the key words. Thus, the universities were assigned the task of facilitating "indigenisation" or "Africanisation", as the process of asserting national control was labelled. This was a relatively easy task, given the thinness of colonial administration. The more difficult task was producing a large enough cadre for a much broader social agenda that required a much more extensive state presence. This agenda included not only a greater presence of the state beyond the capital but also the management of the economic development process that was, by the wisdom of the time, more interventionist. Over and above these objectives there was also the more politically driven agenda to produce a new educated African who was much more in tune with the culture and the social needs of the continent.

Furthermore, the developmentalist ideologies to which national-ists adhered placed great faith in industrialisation. One central fea-ture of economic development was industrialisation and movement away from the monocultural trade specialisation that imperialism had imposed on each colony. Industrialisation required skilled labour, and institutions of tertiary education were seen as serving this function. Kwame Nkrumah was perhaps the most visionary leader in this link between education, technological mastery, and economic develop-ment. The general understanding in development thinking at the time was that "human capital", or "manpower" as it was called then, was, together with capital accumulation and political stability, central to the process of development. As leading experts in manpower and develop-ment at the time, Harbison and Myers wrote:

> The building of modern nations depends upon the development of people and organization of human activity. Capital, natural resources, foreign aid, and international trade, of course, play important roles in economic growth, but none is more important than manpower. (Harbison and Myers, 1964).

African leaders embraced this understanding and often waxed lyrical about the virtues of the new universities they had established. Thus, Tanzania's Julius Nyerere could refer to academics as the "torch bear-ers of our society and the protectors of the flame" and Ghana's Kwame Nkrumah considered universities as "the academic focus of national life reflecting the social, economic, cultural and political aspirations of the people" (both cited in Banya and Elu, 2001: 5). On the pan-African level, two major conferences on education were held – the first in 1961 in Addis Ababa and the second, a follow-up conference, in Tananarive. The conferences assigned seven roles to African universities (Banya and Elu, 2001: 5):

1. To teach and advance knowledge through research;
2. To maintain adherence and loyalty to world academic stan-dards;
3. To ensure unification of Africa;
4. To encourage elucidation of, and, appreciation for, African cul-ture and heritage, and to dispel misconceptions about Africa, through research and the teaching of African Studies;

5. To train the "whole person" for nation-building;
6. To develop human resources for meeting labour force needs;
7. To evolve over the years, truly African institutions of higher learning dedicated to Africa and its people, yet promoting a bond of kinship to the larger human society and to emphasize science and technology so that the continent could by 1980, produce 60% of its own doctors and agriculturalists.

These ambitions led to massive investments in the education system. Significantly, many African governments were committed to universal primary school education. That the commitment was more than political hot air is demonstrated by the sharp changes in school enrolment numbers. Primary school enrolment increased dramatically. A similar story can be told of other levels of education. While in 1960, the modal year of African independence, there were 5 universities; by 1980 this had dramatically increased to 85 universities and 542,700 students. By 2005 enrolment had risen to 4 million, triple what it was in 1991 and representing "one of the highest regional growth rates in the world for tertiary enrollments, averaging 8.7 percent a year" (World Bank, 2009.) Moreover, according to UNESCO, in 1980, higher education enrolments per 100,000 population averaged 132; by 1995, they had grown to 200. The rapid growth in higher education enrolments, however, still places the region well behind other regions of the world. For example, the enrolments per 100,000 population average around 1,020 in the Arab and Asian countries and 1,500 in Latin America (World Bank, 2009).

State and university conflicts

These dramatic increases in enrolment should not conceal the problems the political order had with universities. The relationships between the state and the universities and their communities have been fraught and tumultuous, to say the least. In the first years of independence, the relationship between the universities and the governments was cordial and warm as African governments viewed universities both as instruments of development and as symbols of national sovereignty and pride. Any visit to African campuses suggested that these universities were highly valued and that considerable resources were invested in the setting up of such universities Nevertheless, the honeymoon between African states and universities did not last long.

There were many sources of conflict between the universities and the new governments. The first was over the reconciliation of one-party rule and academic freedom. The widespread understanding among both Africans and non-Africans was that democracy was a "luxury we could not afford". A considerable amount of intellectual energy was expended to demonstrate that the management of political order in the face of the "revolution of rising expectations" (Huntington, 1968) would demand "hard states" or charismatic leaders who would mobilize all the national resources for development. The repressive politics that followed that logic and became the norm simply left no room for the growth of intellectuals occupying public space. Many spaces that were open (at least theoretically) to intellectuals elsewhere were either erased, infested by spies and sycophants, or simply occupied by the state, sometimes physically so that neither "ivory towers" nor "Olympian detachment" nor "self-imposed" marginalisation were meaningful options.

This conflict was magnified by the penchant of African leaders for assuming the role of a philosopher king and for reducing intellectual work to the incantation of the thought of the leader. Leaders sought to acquire intellectual hegemony by themselves or through advisors constructing intellectual (often unabashedly eponymous) frameworks that would guide the national debates. Nkrumah with his pan-Africanism and Nkrumahism, Nyerere with his Ujamaa, and Kaunda with his humanism are some well-known ideological constructs. Nigeria had its Zikism and irredentism. In many cases, most of the ideological schemes propounded by African leaders were highly idiosyncratic and often so incoherent as to be beyond the comprehension of the propagators themselves. What was one to make of Mobutu's "authenticity" beyond its its sartorial symbols and costly extravaganza? Adhesion to them was not only difficult but also hazardous for those sycophants who diligently sought to follow their leader through infinite twists and turns, as the leader sought to bridge the cavernous gap between the rhetoric of national goals and the reality of predatory self-aggrandisement. As noted by Achebe, being a sycophant was not an easy task:

> Worshiping a dictator … wouldn't be so bad if it was merely a matter of dancing upside down on your head. With practice anyone could learn to do that. The real problem is having no way of knowing from one day to another, from one minute to the next, just what is up and what is down. (Achebe).

The second source of conflict was the conceptualisation of African universities as simply producing the "manpower" to indigenise the civil service. This led to complete misunderstanding of the task that lay ahead and as a consequence, underestimation of the intellectual and political complexity of the processes of development and nation-building. Thus, after the first wave of the African intelligentsia had been absorbed by the state and parastatal bureaucracies and once indigenisation had been achieved, most governments had little argument for continued support for the African universities. New arguments about universities generating knowledge through research for "catching up" and for meeting broader social needs beyond those of the state simply did not register.

The third source of contention was over the "relevance of research" in African universities. Governments often argued that the research was "irrelevant", by which they meant that it was not immediately usable in policy matters. They argued that the new universities should somehow serve "development". By this, many often meant that the focus should be on "applied" knowledge; considering basic and especially critical research as "irrelevant" if not downright subversive of the national effort. In some cases, the "relevance" issue spilled over to question the quality of the education process, with academics insisting on standards and governments insisting on relevance as if these were polar opposites.

The fourth bone of contention was the fact that African governments relied heavily on foreign mentors, admirers, or sycophants for intellectual inspiration or affirmation. Thus, Nyerere had a band of foreign "Fabian socialists" who had easy access to him, in sharp contrast to Tanzanians, who had difficulties seeing Nyerere. Kaunda had John Hatch as a close intellectual associate, who was invited to be the first director of the Institute for Humanism; Nkrumah surrounded himself with pan-Africanists, such as George Padmore and W. E. B. Dubois. In later years, there were European and American "radicals" who were later to appear as peripatetic advisors to a whole range of "progressive" regimes in Africa.

In conclusion, the nationalists in power failed to establish an organic link between the newly minted intelligentsia and the state project of nation-building and development. One feature of the state–intelligentsia relation in Africa has been its conflicted nature (Mkandawire and Codesria, 2005) Consequently, there has been no organic link between the state and its intelligentsia with the exception of Afrikaner nationalism, which moulded solid links with the main Afrikaner universities in the pursuit of their diabolical scheme of apartheid (Mkandawire and Codesria, 2005).

The crisis years

The contradictory positions notwithstanding, the few nationalists who remained in office for some time – the Kaundas, Nyereres, Seretse Khamas, Senghors, Kenyattas, and Bandas – continued for a while to devote considerable resources to the universities into the late 1970s. In most cases, however, the continued material support for the universities stood in stark contrast to the ideological and intellectual repression exercised by the state *vis-à-vis* the universities.

In retrospect, all this notwithstanding, African governments continued supporting universities and indeed university education benefitted from the resource booms of the mid-1970s. However, this support for the universities was to suffer from major shocks. The first was the emergence of a leadership that simply did not understand the institutional and material needs of the universities, let alone the intellectual prerequisites for such an institution.[9] A number of nationalists for whom the universities may have been comprehensible as an institution were assassinated or overthrown, often by armies with strong links to the neo-colonial powers. The Khakhicracy held the universities in much lower esteem. The variegated array of armed dictators had no national or developmental projects that specifically required the deployment of skills from the universities. They definitely did not appreciate the anti-militarism of the universities and the universities' claim for autonomy. Once in a while, the military could understand the potential role of the universities and invested considerable resources in them, as happened in Nigeria. However, they generally failed to place the university expansion in any framework of societal change and development. Soldiers rampaging through campuses, beating and raping students, were quite a frequent occurrence. To be sure, there were academics who accepted the role of sycophant and danced to the military music. Some even went as far as to give intellectual gloss to views that were irredeemably nonsensical, incoherent, and self-serving. Eventually, they were hoisted by the petard of their opportunism.

The *coup de grace* was to be delivered by the World Bank in the mid-1980s when it argued that the rate of return on university education

---

9 There is a tale about Idi Amin not understanding why universities wanted to order new books when there were so many in their library already.

was too low. The real shock for higher education was to await structural adjustment programmes. First, with respect to all education, the BWIs insisted on the introduction of "user charges" for access to government schools. The new position of the World Bank was announced at a meeting with African vice-chancellors in Harare in 1986, at which the World Bank argued that higher education in Africa was a misallocation of funds that could be used more productively in other sections of the education system. The case of the World Bank was referred to in a 1988 policy paper on African education, which was "enjoined to limit or moderate enrolment increases by reducing or freezing student intake, to contain costs by lowering expenditures for academic and non-academic staff and student support and by rationalizing programs of study, and, finally, to recover costs through charging tuition, raising fees and initiating student loan schemes" (Banya and Elu, 2001).

During much of the 1980s, the World Bank's view that the rate of return on higher education was lower than that of primary education became the guiding dogma on education policy. The incredible point was that this profound change in policy was based on one study by the World Bank, which in turn was founded on a very weak theoretical and empirical base (Bennell, 1996). Firstly, it is difficult to measure the separate rates of return of different elements of the same system because of the interlinkages and the inseparability among the various elements. Secondly, the focus on individual rates of return ignored the well-established discrepancy of social and private returns, especially for something with a public good character such as education. Furthermore, the rates of return reflected the economic conjuncture. Thirdly, the rates of return of engineers would fall in a stagnating economy. The solution to this problem is not to reduce the training of engineers but to increase the demand for their services, by accelerated investment and the demand for engineers. Finally, to the extent that the Washington Consensus had no vision of the industrialisation of Africa and did not condone any deliberate pursuit of industrial policy, it was natural that governments could not see much use for higher education. At best, the model pushed for the colonial *mise en valeur* trading arrangements and a return to exporting primary products with a minimal state and a limited number of natives to manage the transactions. In such a model, there were no obvious reasons to have lawyers, engineers, architects, etc. Much of this thinking about education was driven by an anti-developmental posture that could not imagine that

African countries might urgently need a wide range of skills.

Although the position was given an air of objectivity by statistical mumbo-jumbo, the main argument lay in the vision that the bank held for Africa and the role of the state in this schema. First, driven by neo-liberal convictions about the negative role of the state in the economy, the World Bank saw no reason for the continued role of the universities in producing the human resources for an expanded role of the state. The international financial institutions imposed conditionalities on the African state that drastically reduced the civil service in many African countries. African governments' end result was that today, Africa is the most under-governed region in the world. The state has been reduced to the colonial *mise en valeur* proportions to maintain law and order and to ensure the exporting of primary commodities. Secondly, having set aside development and especially that based on industrialisation, the World Bank could not see much reason for supporting university education. Economies that resorted to their history of exporting raw materials did not need the wide and complex range of skills associated with industrialisation. As I argued above, the post-independence rapid expansion of tertiary and secondary schools reflected the nationalist ambitions for the industrialisation of Africa and sought to reverse the *mise en valeur* view of colonial development, which, as we noted, did not need much skilled labour. The model of adjustment proposed for Africa did not need a highly skilled labour force, a point that was to be given scientific respectability by the studies on "rates of return" that persuaded many donors to abandon their support for tertiary education and forced governments to cut their support, with disastrous consequences for African economies.

The combined result of repression, this jaundiced view of higher education and fiscal strangulation, fictitious calculus, and blurred vision was criminal neglect of university education. Not only did this lead to the starvation of resources for existing institutions as many donors withdrew from funding higher education, but it also led to a massive brain drain, exacerbating the already dire situation.

The World Bank/UNESCO Task Force on Education had this to say:

> Since the 1980s, many national governments and international donors have assigned higher education a relatively low priority. Narrow – and, in our view, misleading – economic analysis has contributed to the view that public investment in universities and colleges brings

meagre returns compared to investment in primary and secondary schools, and that higher education magnifies income inequality ... As a result, higher education systems in developing countries are under great strain. They are chronically under-funded, but face escalating demand ... (UNESCO, 1998).10

The World Bank report on tertiary education stated:

For nearly two decades, international development assistance has, with few exceptions ... viewed the role of post basic education in Sub-Saharan Africa (SSA) with a blind eye. Pushed by conditionalities and pulled by matching fund requirements, African governments have reluctantly followed suit. In fact, funding priorities— poverty alleviation and millennium development goals— were not wrong, but they were pursued without much attention to associated needs for highly skilled professionals to implement them effectively. As a consequence, official development assistance to postsecondary education in Africa averaged just US$110 million a year between 1990 and 1999, before rising to an average US$51.5 million a year during the 2000 to 2005 period. (World Bank, 2009).

The ease with which African governments accepted some of the crazy ideas about higher education and development in Africa is a reflection not only of the supine position that was the outcome of the need for

---

10. The World Bank elaborates on this point thus: "World Bank investments in education reflected this trend, as the Bank often played an important leadership role in focusing international attention on the poorest of the poor in Africa and elsewhere. As a result, its financing for tertiary education on the continent, which had averaged US$ 103 million annually from FY90-FY94, declined to US$ 30.8 million per year from FY95-FY99, and then rose modestly to US$ 36.6 million per year between FY00 and FY04—in sharp contrast to the positive trends in funding for primary and secondary education. In recent years, Bank funding for tertiary education has continued to rise, but the average of $83.9 million between FY05 to 08, still remains below the levels at the start of the 1990s (see Figure 1). Not surprisingly, the deep decline in Bank funding for tertiary education, particularly for a decade between 1994 and 2004, led many in Africa's education community to conclude that the World Bank was an active opponent of tertiary education" (World Bank, 2009).

financial support to deal with the economic crisis but also of the exhaustion of the nationalist–developmentalist ideology that had been the normative anchor of the post-colonial educational efforts. With respect to primary education, the earlier questions for universal primary education not only to meet international standards but to give the new nationals the socialisation necessary for national cohesion now lost much of their urgency.

Renewed interest and donor manpower needs

While continuing to undermine or marginalise the university system, the donors engaged in increased intervention in policy making, and were faced with a greater need for expatriate and local expertise for feasibility studies, monitoring projects, and evaluating projects. This increased the need for consultancies, which were to tie large numbers of highly qualified people to activities that, while financially lucrative, were ultimately humiliating and intellectually debilitating. The expansion of NGOs also created new demand for university-educated personnel.

This "consultancy industry" attracted a significant amount of human resources, mostly from the university system. The impact of this on research was disastrous. NGOs bent on quick, micro-level issues did not encourage long-term research. One other consequence was that local actors could no longer have access to some of the best expertise without the mediation of donors. The local actors, including the state, were simply priced out of this market. Even in universities, the meagre research funds went unused because one was better off carrying out contract research.

Most significantly, the World Bank, apparently with the help of UNESCO, began to acknowledge the "growing salience of tertiary education" apparently on the basis of "a wealth of recent research (that) has convincingly established the relationship of the accumulation of physical capital and total factor productivity (the combined increase in the productivity of capital and labour) to growth." (World Bank, 2009: xx). Thus it took three decades for the Bank to remove its pernicious and destructive ideological blinkers and see a basic and commonsensical tenet of development economics about the role of human capital in the process of economic development and structural change, as the quote of Harbison and Mysers (1964) above, from the 1960s, clearly shows.

SOME CONSEQUENCES OF MALADJUSTMENT

The dire consequences of adjustment are widely recognised and I need not remind the audience here of what befell their places of teaching and learning.

The problem of quality

Quite remarkably, enrolment in African universities grew rapidly. Consider the following: during the 1994–2000 period, there were 2.5 million new students. Between 2000 and 2006, the total number of students increased from 6.0 million to 9.3 million. However, compared with other parts of the world, these figures represent enrolment ratios that leave Africa far behind other developing countries. Nevertheless, such a rapid increase took place under conditions of limited resources available to institutions of higher learning, with the result that the public expenditure per tertiary student fell from US$6,800 in 1980 to US$1,200 in 2002, and recently averaged just US$981 in 33 low-income SSA countries. All this caused a fall in the ratio of academic staff to students, overcrowded classrooms, and "unrelenting workloads" for teaching staff. Related to the low levels of resources allocated to tertiary education was the low level of funding for scientific research. The World Bank reports that quantitatively, South Africa alone accounted for nearly two-thirds of the region's R&D expenditures.

One current metric of quality is the universities' position in university league tables. Though many academics are highly sceptical of the integrity and scientific validity of these tables, there can be no doubt that they pay attention to them, even if surreptitiously, so I paid attention too. In the Shanghai Academic Ranking of World Universities, only Cape Town appeared among the top 300 and only 2 other South African universities made the top 500. In the QS ranking on the website, there was no African university among the top 100.[11]

In another index (the Times Higher Education World University Rankings), in the top 200, only the University of Cape Town and Alexandria University are named. China had 7 universities, Korea 5, and India none. In another index[12] measuring web presence ranking, of the top 20 African universities, 11 were from South Africa.

---

11 http://www.topuniversities.com/university-rankings/world-university-rankings/2010/results.
12 http://www.webometrics.info/top100_continent.asp?cont=africa.

WHAT IS TO BE DONE?

The universities' future is not the exclusive concern of university staff and students. It is a national issue of the highest order. We should continue to campaign to bring the universities back onto the national agenda of social and economic transformations. This task may be easier now because once again university education is on the political agenda. The new middle class now recognises with alarm that the institutions that produce it are in serious crisis. In addition, the economic pauperisation of members of this class means that sending their children to schools abroad is consequently no longer a viable option for many; they are beginning to make political demands related to the quality of education. African governments are increasing their attention, partly in response to the political pressures for greater enrolment figures and high quality in the institutions of higher learning. A visit to some campuses suggests some significant improvements in staff morale and the infrastructure. However, bearing in mind the terrible reversals during the adjustment era and the enormity of the task ahead, we still really have to bring the universities back in.

The losses we suffered during the "Lost Decades" can be reversed through massive corrective action. The Chinese suffered an immense regression in their tertiary education system during the Cultural Revolution. We too endured the terrible period of "Lost Decades". By 2007, China's tertiary-level enrolment rate had reached 21 per cent compared to Africa's 6 percent. In absolute terms, this means that China has more tertiary-level students than the USA. A total of 40 per cent of these students were engineering students, and today China produces more engineers than the USA. The difference now seems to be that while the Chinese have responded to that through massive expansion of their higher education, we are still bogged down with false dichotomies between education for all and greater investment in higher education. Although most donors now admit that they are pushing African governments out of higher education, they are not in a hurry to engage in the redressing of the disastrous consequences of their policies. Our governments, having no clear policy of industrialisation and transformation, seem to have no clue what they would do if they had additional skilled citizens.

Universities have proved much more resilient than was initially feared, largely because of the enormous commitment by both faculty and students. Consequently, we do not have to begin from scratch, as some donors are wont to think. By working through existing universities, expanding their resources and intake, we can achieve a turnaround. The universities are probably one of the most successful institutions in the West and one of the few remnants of the feudal order that still enjoys wide respect and is directly relevant to modern society. It is for this reason that we should look very carefully at the unbridled experimentation with forms of education that the "North" has not dared fool around with.

We should also recall the African scholarly community itself, which has over the years fiercely defended university education. African scholars have also found mutual sustenance through the various research networks that have sustained intellectual activity during an extremely trying period and that are like to play a central role in the revival of the African intellectual community.

The international context has changed in a more favourable way. The second promise comes with the collapse of the "Washington Consensus" and the "voodoo calculus" on which the systematic destruction of the universities was based. In its characteristically disingenuous shifting of blame onto "donors", the World Bank argued for higher education as if this had been its normal and unbending position on the matter. One would never guess that it was its simplistic calculations of the rate of return that had launched the armada against higher education in Africa. The World Bank, in its new incarnation of the "knowledge bank", now says that it is for university education, and as an ally of higher education it now talks about "revitalizing universities in Africa" (World Bank, 1997a) However, the "knowledge" it refers to is quite specific and related more to managerial and development concerns. It is not knowledge that enhances a society's critical capacity for learning and self-evaluation. I must confess that I find the involvement of these financial institutions in higher education worrisome. We noted earlier that the perception of the universities has a lot to do with the overall societal project. Given its past history, African intellectuals are highly suspicious of the World Bank's new interest in education. The strong opposition was illustrated by the suspicions recently voiced by Nigerian academics of the World Bank loan to higher education, and the subsequent public response by the World Bank disclaiming any ulterior motive behind the loan. There is also the avowal by donors that they want "partnerships" and would like to transfer "ownership" of policies to Africans. Such a relationship presupposes that African societies will mobilise their intellectual resources if the new partnerships are meaningful.

Fourth, the struggles for democratisation and the greater freedoms enjoyed by society at large have not only widened the intellectual space for academia and provided respite from the suffocating atmosphere of authoritarianism but also given greater political protection to it as an institution.

Finally there is the renewed interest in higher education. By the 1990s, the IFIs had discovered that their own programmes on elementary education or primary health care required doctors and teachers who were produced in the tertiary system. The provision of clean water and electricity to the poor and their access to markets and services required infrastructure, which in turn required human capital produced in institutions of higher learning. With the economic recovery it is not surprising that there was a multitude of studies suggesting returns for secondary and tertiary education that are higher than at the primary level (Aturupane et al., 1994)!

Furthermore, as the World Bank revived its interest in economic growth, it rediscovered the importance of education in the "catch-up" process :

> We stress human capital in this report because in the context of SSA, it is arguably the stepping-stone to a viable and growth-promoting industrial system. Physical investment and institutions are important complements: the former cannot be efficiently utilized or maintained where technical and managerial skills are lacking, and the latter cannot be engineered or implemented when human capital is scarce and of questionable quality. The salience of human capital is increased by the necessity of moving up the technological ladder in order to diversify into higher-value, knowledge- and research-intensive activities with good longer-term demand prospects. These promise better returns and are less subject to competitive pressures. (World Bank, 2009).

Greater external contacts

Much of scientific knowledge is foreign in terms of both utilisation and ownership. Therefore, we have to aim to obtain it wherever we can. One defining feature of a developmental state is that it actively encourages learning from foreigners, the adaptation of technologies and organizations to local conditions, and the introduction of productive innovations (Bagchi, 2000). Indeed, Bagchi argued that this is "one distinguishing mark of any successful development states in history". He recounted how in Japan the leaders of the Meiji Restoration realised the supreme importance of education in their pursuit of "civilization and enlightenment" – which meant "catching up". Other developmental states have followed a similar path.

Today China has been exemplarily aggressive in acquiring knowledge by hook or by crook. Thus, in addition to the impressive rates in national institutions, China has aggressively entered foreign institutions of learning. China accounts for 16 per cent of the 2.7 million students abroad, i.e. 430,000 students. Many of these Chinese have attained high positions in research institutions in the USA, and in more recent years they have increasingly returned home in response to favourable economic conditions and incentives designed to stem and reverse the drain brain. As well as these initiatives, China is engaged in what has been described as "massive training schemes" for the millions of rural workers coming into the cities (Dahlman, 2009).

It should be clear that Africa must adopt the most aggressive strategies towards harnessing new technologies for knowledge acquisition, enhancement, and dissemination.

Problems of teachers

The situation in Africa today is that the numbers in the tertiary education system are increasing rapidly but there are serious problems regarding quality, due to the lack of staff and supporting infrastructure. Indeed, it seems that while the latter may be easier to redress (with the Internet and its accompanying possibilities), the staffing problem needs special attention. To resolve this, we need a number of top graduate programmes to produce both the faculty and the researchers. It is distressing to note that in the now widespread phenomenon of ranking world universities, only South Africa has universities among the top two hundred universities in the world. I believe the large countries, such as Nigeria and South Africa, ought to set up top-notch graduate programmes that can provide training in many areas for other African countries. This they can do in a way that recovers costs. Africans are already paying to visit all kinds of places.

The major task as I see it is for the continent to sustain a number of top-class universities to produce a research-grounded faculty for the burgeoning university population. The World Bank estimated that to maintain the current student–teacher ratio (20 students for 1 instructor], the number of instructors would have to increase from approximately 456,000 in 2006 to 908,000 in 2015. Taking account of retirements and other departures, estimated at 20 per cent for the period 2006–15, this will require the recruitment and training of approximately 566,000 new instructors over the period. In the case of Africa's approximately 30 low-income countries, roughly 270,000 new instructors would be required in the period 2006–15, which implies twice as many annual hirings as in the period 2000–06. Since in many countries the student–teacher ratio is hardly conducive to adequate instruction by international standards, it is doubtful that the countries concerned would be able to recruit and train so many instructors even if the necessary financial resources were available.

The report continues:

> However, it will be even harder for those countries to employ a sufficient number of senior faculty members (namely, professors and assistant professors), who are necessary for undertaking research, raising the scientific and pedagogical level of other instructors, and preparing future generations of instructors and research scientists. In fact, information available on approximately 10 countries in the region indicates that the proportion of senior faculty members is on average under 20 per cent, in some cases considerably … In view of the low level of investment in research in Africa, it is doubtful that enough doctoral students can be trained to redress that situation (World Bank, 2009: 35).

I believe that the large countries and some of the older universities can play a key role by improving their PhD programmes and opening them to other countries. South African universities are already playing this role, and I believe that countries such as Ghana can also do so. This they need not do on grounds of charity. They can recuperate the costs of such programmes by charging the full cost of study.

The problem of the brain drain

One of the consequences of the "Lost Decades" was a massive brain drain. We can turn that calamity around into a "brain gain". According to ECA, some 27,000 African intellectuals emigrated to developed countries between 1960 and 1975. Between 1985 and 1990, the number jumped to 60,000, and has averaged 20,000 annually ever since. Both the Addis Ababa and the Lusaka meetings called on African governments to improve the conditions for indigenous professionals and harness their skills better for development. One important role the universities can play is reversing the brain drain or at least facilitating access to African brains abroad. We know that for professional and personal reasons many of the African brains abroad are unlikely to return. Many other parts of the world have responded by devising ways of utilising this brain power, including dual professorships, short-term teaching visits, distant mentoring of individual students, etc.

The experience of East Asia is that Diasporas can be an important source of access to knowledge and that the brain drain can be reversed. I believe that in Africa we have been too passive in addressing the problem of the drain. What is clear today is that countries exploit their Diasporas in various ways. "Visiting professionals" or "sabbaticals" taken at home have become quite widespread in other countries.[13]

Africa's triple challenge is to create states that are developmental and capable of guiding catch-up processes in the many areas in which the continent lags behind, which are democratically elected and pursuing policies that are socially inclusive. This is a tall order that will demand organisational and intellectual capacity and political imagination and will. Such a social order will require a vibrant intellectual community that feeds from and into a vibrant civil society, which in turn engages a democratically responsive state that deploys both human and material resources for development. If in addition to all this we allow ourselves to imagine an industrialised and technologically capable Africa, we will require the universities to be brought back in.

---

13. I once heard an official of the Chinese Academy inform a UNESCO meeting that China was planning more than 15 new MITs. When asked where they would find the teaching staff, she replied that they had enough Chinese teachers in the USA and that they would pay them enough to attract them home. India has Institutes of Technology that seem to be doing the same.

REFERENCES

Abramovitz, Moses. 1995. Elements of Social Capability, in B. H. Koo and D. H. Perkins, *Social Capability and Long-Term Economic Growth*. London: Macmillan, 19-47.

___. 1986. Catching up, Forging Ahead, and Falling Behind. *Journal of Economic History* XLVI, 406.

Acemoglu, D., S. Johnson and James Robinson. 2001. The Colonial Origins of Comparative Development. *American Economic Review.*.

Akyüz, Yilmaz. 2006. *From Liberalisation to Investment and Jobs: Lost in Translation*. Third World Network (TWN).

___. 1996. The Investment-Profit Nexus in East Asian Industrialisation. *World Development*, 24(3), 461-70.

Akyüz, Yilmaz, Ha-Joon Chang and Richard Kozul-Wright. 1998. New Perspectives on East Asian Development. *Journal of Development Studies*, 34(6), 4-36.

Amsden, Alice H. 1985. The State and Taiwan's Economic Development, in P. B. Evans, T. Skocpol and D. Rueschemeyer, *Bringing the State Back In*. Cambridge: Cambridge University Press.

Arrighi, Giovanni. 1973. International Corporations, Labour Aristocracies, and Economic Development in Tropical Africa, in G. Arrighi and J. Saul, *Essays on the Political Economy of Africa*. New York.

Aturupane, Harsha, Paul Glewwe and Paul Isenman. 1994. Poverty, Human Development, and Growth: An Emerging Consensus? *The American Economic Review*, 84(2), 244.

Bach, Daniel C. 2011. Patrimonialism and Neopatrimonialism: Comparative Trajectories and Readings. *Commonwealth & Comparative Politics*, 49(3), 275-94.

Bagchi, A. K. 2000. The Past and the Future of the Developmental State. *Journal of World Systems Research*, 6(2), 398.

Banya, K. and J. Elu. 2001. The World Bank and Financing Higher Education in Sub-Saharan Africa. *Higher Education*, 42(1), 1-34.

Bennell, P. 1996. Using and Abusing Rates of Return: A Critique of the World Bank's 1995 Education Sector Review. *International Journal of Educational Development*, 16(3), 235-48.

Bird, Graham and Dane Rowlands. 1997. The Catalytic Effect of Lending by the International Financial Institutions. *The World Economy*, 20(7).

Bolt, Jutta and Dirk Bezemer. 2008. Understanding Long-Run African Growth: Colonial Institutions or Colonial Education? *Journal of Development Studies*, 45(1), 24-54.

Bourguignon, François. 2004. *The Poverty-Growth-Inequality Triangle*, Indian Council for Research on International Economic Relations, New Delhi.

Breisinger, Clemens and James Thurlow. 2008. *Asian-Driven Resource Booms in Africa: Rethinking the Impacts on Development*. Washington DC: IFPRI.

Caldentey, Esteban Pérez. 2008. The Concept and Evolution of the Developmental State. *International Journal of Political Economy*, 37(3), 27-53.

Carmody, Pádraig. 2009. An Asian-Driven Economic Recovery in Africa? The Zambian Case. *World Development*, 37(7), 1197-207.

Castells, Manual. 1992. Four Asian Tigers with a Dragon Head: A Comparative Analysis of the State, Economy and Society in the Asian Pacific Rim, in R. Henderson and J. Applebaum, *State and Development in the Asian Pacific Rim*. London: Sage Publications, 33-70.

Chang, Ha-Joon. 2002. *Kicking Away the Ladder : Development Strategy in Historical Perspective*. London: Anthem.

Chang, Ha-Joon and Peter Evans. 2000. *The Role of Institutions in Economic Change*. Paper prepared for the meetings of the "Other Canon" group, Venice, Italy and Oslo, Norway.

Chenery, Hollis B., C. Ahluwalia, J. Bell, J. Foluy and Richard Jolly. 1974. *Redistribution with Growth*. London: Oxford University Press for the World Bank.

Collier, P. 2007. The Bottom Billion: Why the Poorest Countries Are Failing and What Can Be Done About It. *Bulletin of the World Health Organisation*, 85(11).

Collier, Paul and Jan W. Gunning. 1999. Why Has Africa Grown Slowly? *Journal of Economic Perspectives, 13(3), 3-22.*

Commission for Africa. 2005. *Our Common Interest.* London: Cabinet Office.

Cruz, Moritz and Bernard Walters. 2008. Is the Accumulation of International Reserves Good for Development? *Cambridge Journal of Economics,* 32, 665-81.

Dahlman, Carl. 2009. Growth and Development in China and India; the Role of Industrial and Innovation Policy in Rapid Catch/Up, in M. Cimoli, G. Dosi and J. E. Stiglitz, *Industrial Policy and Development.* Oxford: Oxford University Press, 303-35.

Daudey, E. and C. García-Peñalosa. 2007. The Personal and the Factor Distributions of Income in a Cross-Section of Countries. *Journal of Development Studies,* 43(5), 812-29.

Deyo, F.C. 1989. *Beneath the Miracle: Labor Subordination in the New Asian Industrialism.* Berkeley.

Easterly, William and Ross Levine. 1995. *Africa's Growth Tragedy.* Washington, D.C.: World Bank.

Estache, Antonio. 2005. *What Do We Know About Sub-Saharan Africa's Infrastructure and the Impact of Its 1990s Reforms?,* Washington DC: The World Bank and ECARES, Université Libre de Bruxelles.

Evans, Peter. 1995. *Embedded Autonomy: States and Industrial Transformation.* Princeton NJ: Princeton University Press.

Evans, Peter. 2004. Development as Institutional Change: The Pitfalls of Monocropping and Potentials of Deliberation. *Studies in Comparative International Development* 38: 30-52.

Figueira, Fernando. 2007. The Latin American Social States: Critical Junctures and Critical Choices, in Y. Bangura, *Democracy and Social Policy.* Basingstoke: Palgrave.

Fischer, Stanley, Ernesto Hernàndez-Catà, and Mohsin S. Khan. 1998. *Africa: Is this the Turning Point.* World Bank, Washington DC.

Garuda, Gopal. 2000. The Distributional Effects of IMF Programs: A Cross-Country Analysis. *World Development,* 28(6), 1031-51.

Gerschenkron, Alexander. 1962. *Economic Backwardness in Historical Perspective.* Cambridge Mass: Harvard University Press.

Harbison, F. and C. Myers. 1964. *Education, Manpower, and Economic Development: Strategies of Human Resource Development.* New York: McGraw-Hill, Inc.

Hausmann, R., L. Pritchett and D. Rodrik. 2005. Growth Accelerations. *Journal of Economic Growth,* 10(4), 303-29.

Herbst, Jeffrey. 2004. Let Them Fail: State Failure in Theory and Practice. *When States Fail. Causes and Consequences.* Princeton NJ. Pp.302-318.

_____. 1990. War and the State in Africa. *International Security* 14: 117-139.

Hirschman, Albert. 1981. The Rise and Decline of Development Economics, in A. Hirschman, *Essays in Trespassing: Economics to Politics and Beyond.* Cambridge: Cambridge University Press,

Hirschman, Albert and M. Rothschild. 1973. Changing Tolerance for Income Inequality Development. *Quarterly Journal of Economics,* 87(4).

Huntington, Samuel. 1968. *Political Order in Changing Societies.* New Haven, Conn.: Yale University Press.

IEG. 1999. *Capacity Building in the Agriculture Sector in Africa.* Washington, D.C.: World Bank.

ILO. 1972. *Employment, Incomes and Equality: A Strategy for Increasing Productive Employment in Kenya.* ILO: Geneva.

IMF. 2004. *Public Investment and Fiscal Policy.* Washington DC: IMF.

Independent Evaluation Group (IEG). 2007. *World Bank Assistance to Agriculture in Sub-Saharan Africa; an IEG Review.* Washington DC: World Bank.

Koo, H. and Eun Mee Kim. 1992. The Developmental State and Capital Accumulation in South Korea, in R. Henderson and J. Applebaum, *State and Development in the Asian Pacific Rim.* Newbury Park: Sage Publications, 121-49.

Kuznets, Simon. 1955. Economic Growth and Income Inequality. *American Economic Review,* 45(1), 1-28.

Leftwich, A. 1994. Goverance, the State and the Politics of Development. *Development and Change,* 25(2).

Lewis, W. A. 1954. Development with Unlimited Supplies of Labour. *The Manchester School,* 22(2), 139-91.

Lipset, Seymour M. 1959. Some Social Requisites of Democracy: Economic Development and Political Legitimacy. *American Political Science Review,* 53 (March).

Madavo, Callisto and Jean-Louis Sarbib. 1997. Africa on the Move: Attracting Private Capital to a Changing Continent. *The SAIS Review* 7: 111-126.

Mezui, Cédric Achille Mbeng and Uche Duru. 2013. *Holding Excess Foreign Reserves Versus Infrastructure Finance – What should Africa do?* African Development Bank Group, Tunis.

Mkandawire, Thandika. 2010. *Running While Others Walk.* Africa Development.

___. 2009a. From the National Question to the Social Question. *Transformation: Critical Perspectives on Southern Africa,* 69(1), 130-60.

___. 2009b. *Institutional Monocropping and Monotasking in Africa.* Geneva: UNRISD,

___. 2004. Disempowering New Democracies and the Persistence of Poverty, in M. Spoor, *Globalisation, Poverty and Conflict.* Dordrecht: Kluwer Academic Publishers, 117-53.

___. 2001. Thinking About Developmental States in Africa. *Cambridge Journal of Economics,* 25(3), 289-313.

___. 1999. Shifting Commitments and National Cohesion in African Countries, in L. Wohlegemuth, S. Gibson, S. Klasen and E. Rothchild, *Common Security and Civil Society in Africa.* Uppsala: Nordiska Afrikainstitutet, 14-41.

Mkandawire, Thandika and Codesria. 2005. African Intellectuals and Nationalism, in T. Mkandawire, *African Intellectuals: Rethinking Politics, Language, Gender and Development.* London and New York: Zed Books.

Moene, K. O. and M. Wallerstein. 2003. *Social Democracy as a Development Strategy.* University of Oslo.

Mosley, Paul and John Weeks. 1993. Has Recovery Begun? Africa's Adjustment in the 1980s Revisited. *World Development,* 21(10), 1583-606.

Myrdal, Gunnar. 1957. *Economic Theory and Underdeveloped Regions.* London: Gerald Duckworth and Co.

Polanyi, Karl. 1946. *The Great Transformation: The Political and Economic Origins of Our Time.* Beacon Press: Boston.

Price, Gregory. 2003. Economic Growth in a Cross-Section of Nonindustrial Countries: Does Colonial Heritage Matter for Africa. *Review of Development Economics,* 7(3), 478-95.

Przeworski, Adam and James Vreeland. 2000. The Effects of IMF Programs on Economic Growth. *Journal of Development Economics,* 62, 385-421.

Ramachandran, M. 2006. On the Upsurge of Foreign Exchange Reserves in India. *Journal of Policy Modeling,* 28(7), 797-809.

Rodrik, Dani. 2006. The Social Cost of Foreign Exchange Reserves. *International Economic Journal,* 20(3).

___. 2001. *The Global Governance of Trade as if Development Really Mattered,* Cambridge, MA: UNDP.

Rostow, W. W. 1960. *The Stages of Economic Growth: A Non-Communist Manifesto.* Cambridge, Massachusetts: Harvard University Press.

Sachs, Jeffrey and Warner Andrew. 1997. Sources of Slow Growth in African Economies. *Journal of African Economies,* 6(3), 335-76.

Sen, Amartya. 2003. *What's the Point of a Development Strategy?.* SSRN eLibrary. London: The Suntory and Toyota International Centres for Economics and Related Disciplines, London School of Economics and Political Science,

Sen, Amartya Kumar. 1999a. Democracy as a Universal Value. *Journal of Democracy,* 10(3).

___. 1999b. *Development as Freedom*. Oxford: Oxford University Press.

Sender, John. 1999. Africa's Economic Performance: Limitations of the Current Consensus. *Journal of Economic Perspectives*, 13(3), 89-114.

Stein, Howard. 2004. *The World Bank and the IMF in Africa: Strategy and Routine in the Generation of a Failed Agenda*. Center for Afro-American and African Studies (CAAS) and School of Public Health, University of Michigan.

Stone, Randall. 2004. Political Economy of IMF Lending in Africa. *American Political Science Review*, 98(4).

Taylor, Lance. 1997. Editorial: The Revival of the Liberal Creed - the IMF and the World Bank in a Globalized Economy. *World Development*, 25(2), 145-52,19.

UNCTAD. 2008a. *Economic Development in Africa: Export Performance Following Trade Liberalization: Some Patterns and Policy Perspectives*. Geneva: United Nations.

___. 2008b. *World Investment Report 2008: Transnational Corporations and the Infrastructure Challenge*. Geneva: United Nations.

___. 2000. *Capital Flows and Growth in Africa*. Geneva: United Nations.

UNCTAD/UNIDO. 2011. Economic Development, in *Report 2011 Africa: Fostering Industrial Development in Africa in the New Global Environment*.

UNESCO. 1998. *World Education Report*. Paris: UNESCO.

UNIDO. 2009. Breaking in and Moving up; New Industrial Challenges for the Bottom Billion and the Middle Income Countries. *Industrial Development Report* 2009. Vienna: United Nations Industrial Development Organisation.

Van de Walle, Nicolas. 2001. *African Economies and the Politics of Permanent Crisis, 1979-1999*. New York: Cambridge University Press.

Wade, Robert. 1991. *Governing Markets: Economic Theory and the Role of Government in East Asian Industrialisation*. London: Macmillan.

Weisbrot, Mark, Robert Naiman and Joyce Kim. 2000. The Emperor Has No Growth: Declining Economic Growth Rates in the Era of Globalisation. http// www.ccerprnet/images/imf/the_emperor has no growth.htm: Center for Economic and Policy Research (CEPR),

Weyland, Kurt Gerhard. 2004. Assessing Latin American Neoliberalism: Introduction to a Debate. *Latin American Research Review*, 39(3), 143-49.

Woo-Cumings, Meredith ed. 1999. *The Developmental State*. Ithaca NY: Cornell University Press.

World Bank. 2010. *Financing Higher Education in Africa*. Washington DC.

___. 2009. *Accelerating Catch-up Tertiary Education for Growth in Sub-Saharan Africa*. Washington DC: World Bank.

___. 2006. *World Development Report: Equity and Development*. Washington DC: Oxford University Press.

___. 2005. *Economic Growth in the 1990s, Learning from a Decade of Reform*. Washington D.C.: World Bank.

___. 2004. *World Bank Report 2004: Making Services Work for Poor People*. Washington DC: World Bank.

___. 1997a. *Revitalising Universities in Africa: Strategy And Guidelines*. Washington DC: World Bank.

___. 1997b. *World Development Report 1997: The State in the Changing World*. New York: Oxford University Press.

___. 1993. *The East Asian Miracle: Economic Growth and Public Policy*. Washington, D.C.: World Bank.

___. 1989. *Sub-Saharan Africa: From Crisis to Sustainable Growth*. Washington, D.C.: World Bank.

___. 1981. *Accelerated Development in Sub-Saharan Africa: An Agenda for Action*. Washington, D.C.: World Bank.

You, Jong-Il. 1998. Income Distribution and Growth in East Asia. *Journal of Development Studies*, 34(6), 37-65.

PROFESSOR THANDIKA MKANDAWIRE: A PROFILE

Professor Thandika Mkandawire is the first to hold the Chair in African Development at the London School of Economics and Political Science (LSE). He is also the Olof Palme Professor for Peace with the Institute for Future Studies in Stockholm. He has been the Director of the United Nations Research Institute for Social Development and Director of the Council for the Development of Social Science Research in Africa (CODESRIA). He was a Senior Research Fellow at the Centre for Development Research in Copenhagen and has taught at the Universities of Stockholm and Zimbabwe. His research interests include development theory, economic policy, development and social policy in developing countries, and the political economy of development in Africa.

Printed in the United States
By Bookmasters